PHILIP YANCEY

PRAYING WITH THE KGB

A STARTLING REPORT FROM A SHATTERED EMPIRE

MULTNOMAH

Portland, Oregon

Unless otherwise indicated, all Scripture references are from the Holy Bible: New International Version, copyright 1973, 1978, 1984 by the International Bible Society. Used by permission of Zondervan Bible Publishers.

Edited by Liz Heaney
Cover design by Bruce DeRoos

PRAYING WITH THE KGB
© 1992 by Philip Yancey
Published by Multnomah Press
10209 SE Division Street
Portland, Oregon 97266

Multnomah Press is a ministry of
Multnomah School of the Bible
8435 NE Glisan Street
Portland, Oregon 97220

Printed in the United States of America.

Library of Congress Cataloging-in-Publication Data

(CIP information not available at time of printing.)

92 93 94 95 96 97 98 99 00 01 - 10 9 8 7 6 5 4 3 2

What People Are Saying about *Praying with the KGB*

"Brilliantly crafted, as is everything Philip Yancey writes. This book is a thrilling testimony to the power of God's Spirit to overcome even the most powerful of human empires—and a testimony to the faithfulness of God's people in a land of oppression."

Charles W. Colson
Chairman, Prison Fellowship
Noted Author and Speaker

"A wonderful book! I missed dinner when I read it because I couldn't put it down."

Charles R. Swindoll
Senior Pastor, Evangelical Free Church,
Fullerton, California
Award-winning Author

"I was captivated and deeply moved by the events recorded in this book—events that would have been unthinkable a few years ago. This compelling account powerfully reminded me of Who is ultimately in control—no matter how desperate the situation may seem. *Praying with the KGB* is one of those rare I-just-couldn't-put-it-down books. But when you have, you'll find your faith strengthened to face the "KGBs" of your own life."

Bruce Wilkinson
President, Walk Thru the Bible Ministries, Inc.

"*Praying with the KGB* is the most incredible story I have read in a decade. I could barely read a chapter without tears of wonder, joy, and worship streaming down my face. As the Christian Bridge delegation met with the leaders of the KGB, the Journalists Club, the Zagorsk prison, the Academy of Social Sciences—and an ex-con named Basil—I felt as if I should take off my shoes and fall on my face for it seemed I was standing on holy ground."

Neta Jackson
Author

"Philip Yancey's captivating style kept me intrigued from beginning to end. Every recorded change from the former Communist regime, every description of the sadness of the land and its people, stays etched in the mind through his crisp, transparent amazement."

Stephen Hayner
President, InterVarsity

Contents

Of all that was done in the past, you eat the fruit, either rotten or ripe. . . . For every ill deed in the past we suffer the consequence.

— *T. S. Eliot*

CHAPTER ONE

Invitation to a Revolution

A memory from childhood: An eye injury has kept me home from school, and all day I must lie still on the couch, with dark patches covering both eyes. My mother is ironing, and the hot, sour smell of pressed cotton fills the room. The radio, perpetually tuned to a Christian station, sends out a stream of string-heavy hymn arrangements until noon, when a gruff, familiar voice comes on. "Friends, it's Carl McIntire. Have you heard that Khrushchev claims to want peace? Sure,

Khrushchev wants peace. A piece of this, a piece of that, until he has it all!"

I grew up nourished on fear in a hotbed of southern conservatism. An uncle, warning of Communist infiltration, packed up his family and moved to Australia. When the newspaper ran a photo of Khrushchev pounding his shoe on the table with the chilling caption, "We will bury you!" I took the threat literally. I practiced crawling under my school desk with my hands over my head, in the position we were to assume if Castro ever launched the nuclear missiles aimed our way. For the school science fair, I debated which model bomb shelter to build.

In the tenth grade, using money from my paper route, I purchased one hundred copies of a scary book called *None Dare Call It Treason* which I then distributed free to my classmates, like gospel tracts. Church further fed the fear. There I heard of Russian Christians condemned to slave labor in Siberian salt mines, and of martyrs in China who declared their faith just before the Communists chopped off their heads. "What will you say when the Communists take over here?" the pastor challenged us. "Will you confess Christ as Lord even if it means prison or death? Or will you deny him and compromise?"

I read somewhere that the Communists examined the hands of their conquered foes for calluses: Uncallused bourgeoisie they lined up and shot; those with worker hands they set free. I raked leaves with a passion, scorning gloves in order to coax the resulting blisters into calluses. I also read that Communists spared anyone who spoke their language. My brother signed up for Russian classes and I studied Chinese, in the hope that one family member would survive an enemy assault from either direction.

Over the years, my politics mellowed and my fear subsided. Even so, nagging doubts remained—do any of us shake off the strangling fears of childhood? Every few years, until recently, *Time* magazine printed a map showing the global advance of world communism and each time, it seemed, the page got redder and redder. And just when I thought I had overcome my childhood hysteria, I read all three volumes and 1877 pages of *The Gulag Archipelago* by Alexander Solzhenitsyn. Was Carl McIntire right after all?

It was against this background that I received an invitation to go to Moscow with a group called Project Christian Bridge. The letter, signed by the chairman and four other members of the Supreme Soviet, could, except for the flawed grammar and misquoted Bible reference, have been written by an American evangelist.

> In the difficult, often agonizing transitional period that our country is experiencing . . . spiritual and moral values acquire a great, if not paramount significance in their ability to guarantee us against confrontation, civil conflicts, the erosion of moral foundations, and the lowering of standards. . . .
>
> We know the role which your Christian organizations are playing as you following the great words of Christ: 'Faith without works is dead.' You are able to assist in the social development of a country and you are able to establish friendly relations with other countries, including the Soviet Union.
>
> All of this has caused us to address you with words of brotherhood and cooperation. We are certain that Soviet people, like American people, share a common striving for the ideas of humanism, cleansing from filth, the celebration of good, love, and charity between our people and between all people of the world. We are charging the prominent Christian activist Mikhail Morgulis to act as

НАРОДНЫЙ ДЕПУТАТ СССР

НАРОДНИЙ ДЕПУТАТ СРСР	ССРИ ХАЛГ ДЕПУТАТЫ	ДЕПУТАТИ ХАЛҚИН СССР
НАРОДНЫ ДЭПУТАТ СССР	TSRS LIAUDIES DEPUTATAS	ԽՈՐՀՐԴԱՅԻՆ ՊԱՏԳԱՄԱՎՈՐ
СССР ХАЛАК ДЕПУТАТИ	ДЕПУТАТ АА ПОПОРУУЙЙ АА УИНУНИЯ РСС	
СССР ХАЛЫҚ ДЕПУТАТЫ	PSRS TAUTAS DEPUTĀTS	СССР-ик ХАЛА ДЕПУТАТЫ
ᲡᲡᲠ ᲯᲐᲠᲮᲝᲕᲘᲡ ᲣᲛᲐᲦᲚᲔᲡᲘ ᲨᲔᲯᲣᲚᲔᲑᲐ	СССРАВ ЭА ДЕПУТАТЫ	NSV LIIDU RAHVASAADIK

◄ 1989—1994 гг. ►

19 сентября 1991 г. _____19__г.

ОБРАЩЕНИЕ

К лидерам христианских движений США

Мы обращаемся к вам от имени народных депутатов СССР, которые принимали активное участие в подготовке и проведении через Верховный Совет СССР Закона о свободе совести в СССР, как и других Законов в области прав человека - свободе печати, передвижения, общественных и политических организаций, судебной защиты достоинства, чести и собственности личности. В переживаемый нашей страной трудный, нередко мучительный переходный период от тоталитарной системы к парламентаризму, рыночной экономике, открытому обществу огромное, быть может, первостепенное значение приобретают духовные, нравственные ценности, способные гарантировать нас от конфронтации, гражданских конфликтов, размывания моральных устоев, падения нравов.

Мы знаем о той роли, которую играют ваши религиозные организации, которые руководствуются великими словами Христа: "Вера без дел мертва", что помогает вам вносить свой значительный вклад в общественное развитие страны, в становление дружеских отношений с другими странами, в том числе Советским Союзом.

Все это побуждает нас обратиться к вам со словами братства и сотрудничества. Мы уверены, что у советских людей, как и у американцев, есть общее стремление к идеалам гуманизма, очищения от скверны, к торжеству добра, любви и милосердия между нашими народами, между всеми народами земного шара. Мы поручаем в качестве нашего посланника и посредника выдающемуся христианскому деятелю Михаилу Моргулису донести наши чувства и замыслы о сотрудничестве и взаимной помощи до христианских организаций Америки.

Мы были бы признательны, если бы Конгресс и Администрация США ознакомились с нашим Обращением к христианским организациям вашей страны и содействовали развитию сотрудничества с нашими независимыми общественными организациями, с законодательными и исполнительными органами в целях осуществления нравственных идей, развития фондов милосердия, гражданского общества, культуры, образования в нашей стране.

Мы готовы содействовать организации встреч лидеров христианских движений США с депутатами и руководством Верховного Совета СССР, Президентом нашей страны М.С.Горбачевым, Президентом РСФСР Б.Н.Ельциным, руководителями других союзных республик, население которых привержено нравственным ценностям христианства.

КОНСТАНТИН ЛУБЕНЧЕНКО
Член Верховного Совета СССР,
Президент Ассоциации Парламентариев
ГЕОРГИЙ ШАХНАЗАРОВ
Народный депутат СССР
Помощник Президента СССР

ТАМАРА ТЮРИНА
Член Верховного Совета СССР
СЕРГЕЙ БЕЛОЗЕРЦЕВ
Народный депутат СССР
ИГОРЬ СОРОКИН
Народный депутат СССР

Letter of appeal signed by Konstantin Lubenchenko, Georgii Shakhnazarov, Tamara Tiurina, Sergei Belozertsev, and Igor Sorokin, leaders of the Supreme Soviet.

our envoy and mediator in carrying our feelings and thoughts about cooperation and mutual assistance to Christian organizations in America.

. . . [We wish to] implement moral ideas, to develop charitable funds and civil societies. We are prepared to assist in the meeting of leaders of Christian movements in the USA with deputies and the leadership of the Supreme Soviet of the USSR, President M. S. Gorbachev, President B. N. Yeltsin, and the leaders of other Soviet republics, whose people are devoted to the moral values of Christianity.

What's the catch? I wondered. Why were Communist leaders presenting themselves as concerned about filth, good, love, charity, and "moral foundations"? What did these people truly want from us?

More out of curiosity than anything else, I agreed on short notice to join the ad hoc delegation that included television and radio broadcasters, educators, lawyers, publishers, Russia specialists, pastors, businessmen, and mission executives.* The Soviet government had promised to approve visas overnight and to pick up expenses within the country. It seemed an ideal way to visit Russia, bypassing the red tape that entangles many visitors.

Our delegation rendezvoused in the Frankfurt, Germany, airport in late October 1991. None of us knew what to expect from the trip. Changes were happening at lightning speed in the Soviet Union, making even the immediate future impossible to predict. For example, we had been promised a meeting with Gorbachev, but would he still hold an office by the time we got there? Would the Supreme Soviet, the nation's

* For a complete list of the participants in Project Christian Bridge, see Appendix A on page 91.

parliament and our official hosts, even survive in view of independence demands by fractious republics?

When I returned on November 7, the seventy-fourth anniversary of the Bolshevik takeover, I no longer wondered why the Soviet government had invited a delegation of evangelical Christians. A revolution has taken place in the great, sprawling land that spans eleven time zones, a revolution every bit as sweeping and monumental as the one that few Soviets deigned to commemorate on November 7.

"All history, once you strip the rind off the kernel, is really spiritual," said historian Arnold Toynbee. The recent events in the former Soviet Union demonstrate the truth of his statement. While Western media tend to focus on the economic crisis, wherever we went government officials and private citizens alike affirmed that the true crisis in their nation was moral and spiritual. We heard that opinion expressed so adamantly and so frequently that I came to see it as the great untold story of the USSR—and the reason behind the Soviets' proposal for a linkage called Christian Bridge.

As "guests of the president," our group received VIP treatment: a televised airport reception by government officials, private tours of the Kremlin museums (they literally shut the doors and locked other tourists out), accommodations in one of Moscow's most luxurious hotels, daily feature coverage in the national media, and an itinerary that included meetings with Gorbachev, the Supreme Soviet, *Pravda*, the KGB, Raisa Gorbachev's Culture Fund, the Academy of Social Sciences, and the Journalists' Club. One television producer told us, "Only Armand Hammer has received such treatment here, with access to so many places."

Some members of our delegation came with specific agendas: to obtain official sanction for their religious broadcasts, to speed the process of publishing Christian literature, to establish Christian study programs.

We all hoped our meetings would help promote Christian work in general. Gradually, however, it became clear that we were not "using" the Soviet officials nearly so much as they were using us. Five years ago most of the activities of evangelical Christian organizations would have been illegal; now the government is reaching out to those same organizations in a desperate attempt to stave off societal collapse. The revolution has come that far.

In this communal room, no one is ever bored,
For in the most visible place hangs the portrait of Lenin.
To you, happy children, he opens the whole world,
He looks at us with a big smile, as if about to speak.
Be happy, little ones,
Grandchildren of the October Revolution.
                                    — *Soviet nursery school song*

CHAPTER TWO

Rumblings from the Volcano

I experienced a rude awakening in the Soviet Union, an empire I had always viewed as a threat to take over the world. Granted, its huge stockpile of nuclear weapons poses a unique threat, but who spread the alarming reports that the Soviet economy would soon catch up to the West? Certainly no one who ever has visited there.

My process of disabusal began on the trip over with stories about Aeroflot, the national airline. One veteran of thirty-two Aeroflot flights told me of her surprise on looking down and seeing the runway beneath her feet. Someone had neglected to patch a hole in the fuselage. When she alerted the flight crew, they seemed unconcerned about the outside air rushing in. "See, the windows leak too," they pointed out as if to reassure her. "We won't fly high enough for cabin pressurization to be a problem." When the plane climbed, ice formed in the overhead baggage rack; when it descended, the ice melted, dousing her. She also had no seat belt.

As our plane dipped below the cloud cover on its initial approach into Moscow, I saw black highways threading a design in the late-October snowscape, but where were the vehicles? Comparable highways in Ohio or Pennsylvania would have been clogged with traffic. Eventually I found the vehicles: they formed a line eight blocks long, motors idling, waiting for gasoline.

Once inside Moscow's international airport I asked a question that often would occur to me, "When will they turn on the lights?" Can an entire airport be lit with a single forty-watt bulb? A local explained that Russia was running short of light bulbs.

On the drive into town, two things stood out: shabby construction and long lines of people at every storefront. What kind of society requires all its citizens, plumbers and nuclear physicists alike, to spend two hours a day standing in line? They are herded from place to place like farm animals and made to stand in orderly rows, waiting, waiting, always waiting, for goods no one would buy if they had any other choice.

A weirdly insulated Third World-level economy rests on the backs of an educated, cultured citizenry, all of whom seem clinically depressed. First under serfdom, then under communism, the Russian people have been beaten down. Samuel Johnson once remarked to Boswell, on passing a beggar, "I suppose it's better to have a society in which some are unhappy than one in which none are happy—which would be the case if perfect equality existed." Soviet communism never achieved its goal of perfect equality, but it did achieve the side-effect Johnson predicted. An entire nation has lost its smile.

"Adam and Eve were Russian, you know," begins one joke Russians used to tell on themselves. "It's a logical deduction. They were improperly clothed, possessed only one apple between them, and someone was always telling them they lived in paradise!" Today, the joke needs revising—no one is telling the Russians they live in paradise. No one would dare. A cloud of impending doom hangs in the air.

A visitor gets the feeling of touring an active volcano. Smoke plumes curl from the top, red lava jets out a few places on the sides, but from down deep comes an ominous warning that the entire mountain may soon blow.

The danger is easily sensed beneath the crust of daily life. One day I went shopping. In the Melodia record store in downtown Moscow I chose ten classical albums: a fine selection of piano music, Russian liturgies, and chamber orchestra works, all featuring world-class performers. I waited in three lines, as always: one to place my order, one to pick it up, and one to pay. The bill for the ten albums came to forty rubles—about eighty-five cents at the official exchange rate. ("Did you check to see if they have grooves?" asked another member of our group when I returned to the hotel and announced my prize.)

I invited a friend out to lunch. We chose one of the new free-enterprise grills to insure better quality and service, knowing the prices would be triple those of a state-run restaurant. After a twenty-minute wait in line, we ordered two of everything on the menu: steak, green beans, cranberries, bread and butter, caviar, dessert, beverage. The total came to forty-three cents— for both of us.

Such an economy cannot last. No one can even print a record jacket for eight-and-a-half cents, much less press a record. No one can grow a twenty-cent steak. A twilight-zone economy based on the ruble is now colliding with the economic realities of the rest of the world. Within the insulated Soviet system, the prices make sense. For a middle-class Russian earning three hundred to four hundred rubles per month, my ten albums would represent a few days' salary. But because of government subsidies, prices bear no relation to the actual cost of the product. Soviets pay three rubles for a gallon of gasoline. Meanwhile, an imported pair of Nike running shoes goes for 2500 rubles, more than six months' salary.

Every month the ruble continues its free fall in the world exchange. At the time of our visit the Union was disintegrating, and various republics outside Russia were printing money around the clock as fast as the presses could run. They cared not whether the ruble collapsed, since most republics planned to have their own currencies in place before long. Alongside the volcano, the ground trembled.

And yet despite all these problems it would be a gross distortion to depict only fear and gloom, for a visitor to the former Soviet empire senses far more. Freedom has exploded like a shellburst.

"Throw open the heavy curtains which are so dear to you—you who do not suspect that the day has already dawned outside!" said Solzhenitsyn in 1969. Nowadays, everyone with eyes can see the bright light of dawn. Solzhenitsyn, once proclaimed a traitor and exiled, is now an honored citizen. Cite him in any gathering of intellectuals or even government bureaucrats and heads will nod affirmatively. Sometimes, spontaneous applause breaks out.

"I never thought this could happen, this revolution," said one former dissident. "We are like children waking from a nightmare in the middle of the night. All we want is reassurance that the nightmare won't happen again." No one can give that reassurance for the future, but last fall, at least, the atmosphere was exhilarating. Everywhere—the newspapers, Radio Moscow, vendor stalls, restored churches, street preachers—signs of the new freedom abounded. Our very presence in Moscow, as North American Christians invited to advise the government on spiritual issues, was a token of the new dawn.

It's God that's worrying me. That's the only thing that's worrying me. What if He doesn't exist? What if Rakitin's right—that it's an idea made up by men? Then, if He doesn't exist, man is the chief of the earth, of the universe. Magnificent! Only how is he going to be good without God? That's the question.

— Fyodor Dostoyevsky,
The Brothers Karamazov

CHAPTER THREE
Church Bells in the Kremlin

It would be hard to overstate the chaos we found in the Soviet Union, a nation that was about to shed its historical identity as well as its name. One day the central bank ran out of money. A few days later the second largest republic seceded. A sense of crisis pervaded everything. Doctors announced the finest hospital in Moscow might close its doors in a month—no more cash. Crime was increasing almost fifty percent a year. No one knew what the nation would look like in a year or even six months. Who would control the nuclear weapons? Who would print the currency?

Perhaps because of this chaos, the Supreme Soviet seemed delighted to meet with our delegation. After a full day of listening to rancorous complaints from breakaway republics, an evening with nineteen foreign Christians probably seemed like a recess period.

When the letter proposing Project Christian Bridge went out in September 1991, the Supreme Soviet was the highest governing body in the nation, comparable to the U.S. Congress. By the time we arrived in Moscow, though, barely a month later, no one seemed sure what the Supreme Soviet was supposed to be doing. Five of the twelve republics had not bothered to send delegates. Most major decisions were being handed down as presidential decrees from Mikhail Gorbachev or, more significantly, from Boris Yeltsin of the Russian republic.

We met with twenty committee chairmen and deputies in the Grand Kremlin Palace, a huge building built in the first half of the nineteenth century as a residence for the tsars. The palace, with its chandeliers, frescoed hallways, parquet floors, and decorative plaster moldings, still conveys a fine sense of grandeur. (On the way to the meeting we passed a park where stooped-over Russian women swept snow from the sidewalks with crude brooms of hand-tied straw. The contrast, in an egalitarian state, was stunning.)

The two groups, Supreme Soviet deputies and North American Christians, faced each other across long wooden tables. One end of the meeting room was dominated by a massive painting, in socialist realist style, of Lenin addressing a group of workers in Red Square. His face wore a severe, clench-jawed "we will right the world" expression.

Some of us hardly could believe the deputies' warm welcome. From these very offices in the Grand

Kremlin Palace, over the past seventy years, other Soviet leaders had directed a campaign against God and religion unprecedented in human history. They stripped churches, mosques, and synagogues of religious ornaments, banned religious instruction to children, and imprisoned and killed priests. The government opened forty-four antireligious museums, and published a national newspaper called *The Godless*.

Using government funds, first the League of Militant Atheists and then The Knowledge Society organized "unevangelism" campaigns of lectures and personal witnessing, with the specific aim of stamping out all religious belief. Vigilantes known as the "Godless shock brigades" went after the most stubborn believers. Until the fall of 1990, rigorous atheism had been the official doctrine of the Soviet government.* Now, exactly a year later, nineteen evangelical Christians were sitting across the table from the present leaders.

Konstantin Lubenchenko, chairman of the Supreme Soviet, introduced his side of the table, joking amiably as he came to his vice chairman, a Muslim from the republic of Azerbaijan: "He follows Muhammad, not Jesus. Who knows, someday we may find out we all serve the same God." The vice chairman, who looked like a Turkish body-builder squeezed into a suit two sizes too small, did not smile.

Lubenchenko is a handsome man with an expressive, strong-boned face. He wore his hair swept back from his forehead as if he had run a brush through it once, taking no time for a part. He was gregarious and witty, often interrupting his fellow deputies with jokes and repartee.

* The USSR Freedom of Conscience Law, adopted in October 1990, formally abolished restrictions on religious faith. Article 5 represents the most dramatic change in policy: "The state does not fund religious organizations or activity associated with the propaganda of atheism." Government sponsorship of atheism campaigns are now illegal.

Nine months before, as a newly elected deputy, Lubenchenko had visited the United States to observe democracy in action. He booked a room at the Washington Sheraton the week of the National Religious Broadcasters' Convention, one of the largest gatherings of evangelical Christians. As he stood in the lobby, adrift in a foreign land whose language and customs he did not know, the wife of Alex Leonovich, an NRB delegate, overhead him speaking Russian. The Leonoviches introduced themselves to Lubenchenko. They and Mikhail Morgulis, a Russian emigré, escorted the Soviet visitor around the capital, and invited him to the next day's Presidential Prayer Breakfast, where an awed Lubenchenko met President George Bush and other government leaders.

A friendship developed between Lubenchenko and American Christians, and it was mainly through these contacts that Project Christian Bridge had come about. Just one week before our visit, the Supreme Soviet elected Lubenchenko as its chairman, which guaranteed us a cordial reception.

Our meeting with the deputies opened with brief statements from both sides. Our group, well aware of the ardent antireligious policies pursued by this state government for many years, began rather tentatively. We spoke up for freedom of religion, and asked for the right to distribute Bibles and broadcast religious programs without restrictions.

Lubenchenko waved these opening remarks aside, as if to say, You're preaching to the converted here. "We need the Bibles very much," he said. "Is there a way to distribute them free instead of charging, so more people can get them?" I stole a glance at the mural of Lenin, wondering what he would have thought of these developments in his motherland.

After a few more comments John Aker, a pastor from Rockford, Illinois, spoke up. In preparation for this visit, our delegation members had urged each other to avoid any tone of triumphalism. We should approach the Soviets with respect, not offending them with direct references to the failures of their country. We should be honest about the weaknesses of the United States in general and the American church in particular. In that spirit John Aker remarked on the resurgence of the Soviet church.

"Returning home from my last visit to your country, I flew over the city of Pittsburgh just as the sun was setting to the west," he said. "It was a beautiful sunset, and I photographed it from the window of the plane. As I did so, I realized that the sun was just then rising in the Soviet Union. Going down in America, but coming up on the Soviet Union.

"Please don't be fooled by us tonight. I believe in many ways the sun seems to be going down on the church in America. We have taken too much for granted in our country and we have grown complacent. But I believe the sun is rising on the church here. Re-examine your history. Examine your spiritual legacy. And I pray you will lead your people in that light."

The deputies would have none of it. One commented wryly, "Perhaps the setting sun does not symbolize the decline of the Western church, but rather the sinking of communism in Russia!" Other deputies laughed loudly. Lubenchenko identified the speaker as a major general in charge of the Ministry of State Security.

The general continued, "In the past weeks I have been negotiating reductions in strategic nuclear weapons. I have attended many meetings with my American counterparts. The cuts we have made will make our world more secure, I believe. And yet I must say that this meeting with you Christians tonight is more important for the long-term security of our nation than the meeting between our nations' presidents on eliminating nuclear weapons. Christianity can contribute much to our security as a people."

I checked the translation with the delegate beside me, who spoke Russian. Yes, I had heard right. The general really had said our meeting was more important than the START talks. A deputy from Byelorussia jumped in with warm praise for Christians who had responded so quickly with help for the victims of the Chernobyl disaster. Other deputies nodded assent. Another Soviet asked about the possibility of opening Christian colleges in the USSR.

Our group began to detect a pattern that would become increasingly evident throughout our trip. Whenever we tried to inject a note of realism, our Soviet hosts would cut us off. They looked on the United States, with all its problems, as a shining light of democracy; they saw the Christian church as the only hope for their demoralized citizens.

The Soviet leaders voiced a fear of total collapse and anarchy unless their society could find a way to change at the core, and for this reason they had turned to us for help. Somewhere in government files there must exist a profile of American evangelicals: good citizens, by and large; don't meddle too much in politics; support their leaders; strong work ethic. That citizen profile is sorely lacking in the USSR. And if God must come as part of the package, well, all the better.

One deputy quizzed us on the relationship between democracy and religion. "There is a direct tie," we responded. "Democracy is based on a belief in the inherent dignity of men and women that comes from their being created in the image of God. Furthermore, we also believe that governments are given divine authority to administer justice. In that respect, you leaders are agents of God." The deputies seemed to like that thought.

In general the Soviet deputies seemed bright,

earnest, and deeply concerned about the problems outside the Grand Kremlin Palace. Most were young and
energetic—a good thing, since they had been meeting
thirteen hours straight that day—and I thought it a
shame that these deputies would likely find themselves
shut out of politics as the Soviet Union continued to
unravel.

As the evening grew late, Lubenchenko asked one
of the youngest deputies, an attractive woman in charge
of cultural affairs, to sum up the new attitude toward
religion. "I am impressed with how freely you can talk
about your faith," she said, softly but with deep emo-
tion. "I envy you! We have all been raised on one religion: atheism. We were trained to believe in the material
world and not God. In fact, those who believed in God
were frightened. A stone wall separated these people
from the rest.

"Suddenly we have realized that something was
missing. Now religion is open to us, and we see the
great eagerness of young people. I envy those young
people growing up today who can study religion. This
is a hard time for us, when our ideals have been
destroyed. We must explore religion, which can give us
a new life and a new understanding about life."

When she finished, Mikhail Morgulis, the organizer
of our trip, asked if we could stand and pray. Television
cameramen switched on banks of lights and roamed the
room, poking their camera lenses into the faces of praying Soviet deputies, drinking in this strange sight for the
benefit, and probable bewilderment, of Soviet television
viewers.

On our way out we posed with our hosts for photos in the great hall, and I could not help noticing a
bookstand display featuring the film *Jesus* and copies of
the Bible in Russian. What had happened to the atheistic
state? The change in attitude was unfathomable. I
doubted whether the U.S. Congress would have invited

these same evangelical leaders to consult with them on spiritual and moral values, and I certainly couldn't remember seeing Bibles for sale in the U.S. Capitol building.

We exited the Grand Kremlin Palace, and a chorus of bells rang out in the clear October air. The Revolution had silenced all church bells until a decree from Gorbachev made it legal for them to sound again. I saw an old woman wearing a *babushka* kneeling before a cathedral in prayer, an act that would have required immense courage a few months before. The irony struck me: within the walls of the Kremlin—officially atheistic until 1990—stand five separate gold-domed cathedrals. Is there another seat of government in all the world so crowded with churches?

A guide had pointed out a brick gate in the Kremlin wall still referred to as the "Savior Gate." It got its name from a large gilded frame mounted above the opening in the wall. Before the Revolution the frame held a painting of Jesus; since then, it has hung empty.

I looked at my watch, still set on Chicago time. It was October 31, Reformation Day. The Reformation had not penetrated the borders of Russia, in the sixteenth century or any other century. Now, in the least likely of all places, at the least likely of all times, there were unmistakable signs of spiritual awakening. "It's enough to make you a post-millennialist," muttered one member of our group.

Those men, so powerful,
always shown somewhat from below by crouching cameramen,
who lift a heavy foot to crush me,
no, to climb the steps of the plane,
who raise a hand to strike me,
no, to greet the crowds obediently waving little flags,
those men who sign my death warrant,
no, just a trade agreement
which is promptly dried by a servile blotter . . .
> — Stanislaw Baranczak,
> "Those Men So Powerful"

CHAPTER FOUR
Praying with the KGB

Several times in Moscow we passed the sturdy pedestal which, until the failure of the August coup, had supported a statue of the founder of the secret police. Toppling the statue required the use of a huge crane, and for several days the workmen let the statue of Feliks Dzerzhinsky dangle from a steel-cable noose high above the street, a shocking symbol of the triumph of freedom over fear.

"The suspended statue reminded me of an oversized

crucifix, like you see in South American cities," recalled one observer. "Only this martyr was the destroyer, not the Savior, of our people." By the time we arrived Dzerzhinsky had been dumped unceremoniously in a park by the Moscow River, but Muscovites were still filing solemnly past the bare pedestal, staring at the vacant space, shaking their heads in disbelief.

We too shook our heads in disbelief when we got a friendly invitation to stop by the squat, hulking KGB building behind the pedestal and sip tea with the organization's leaders. Most of us had read dissidents' memoirs that describe in hideous detail what went on inside Lubyanka, the most famed and feared of Moscow's many prisons. From offices above that basement prison the KGB had overseen a vast network of prisons—several of which accommodated over one million inmates—exposed by Solzhenitsyn as "the gulag archipelago."

I felt long-buried rancor rush to the surface as we discussed our visit to the KGB. Cautious historians put the death toll from the camps and purges at 10 to 20 million; Solzhenitsyn reckons the figure at 60 to 70 million. I can hardly comprehend these numbers, but I recoil in disgust against accounts of simple human cruelty inflicted by the KGB.

Andrei Sakharov records that agents put cockroaches in his mail envelopes, punctured tires, smeared windows with glue, and stole his dental bridges, glasses, and toothbrush. Solzhenitsyn writes of a friend who got a twenty-five-year prison sentence for attending the secret reading of a novel. It is rare to meet a Russian whose family has not been directly affected by KGB cruelty. Now we were to sip tea with the authors of such brutishness?

Some in our group, veterans of Iron Curtain days, had told us stories of harassment by KGB informers, and we had joked about wiretaps in our hotel, formerly the nest of the Central Committee of the Communist party. That very day a man had approached two of us on Red Square and asked a few harmless questions, feigning drunkenness. We met him again in the lobby of the KGB building; recognizing us, he turned and ducked into a hallway. Unlike the statue of its founder, the KGB had not simply disappeared.

And, though toppled from his pedestal outside, even Feliks Dzerzhinsky lived on inside the KGB headquarters. The room we met in had a large photo of him still hanging on one wall, along with the obligatory photo of Lenin. The wood-paneled room was arranged like a small auditorium, with long tables oriented toward a speaker's table at the end. A handful of KGB agents, their faces as blank and impassive as their movie stereotypes, stood at attention by the doorway.

An aide to Gorbachev made a few opening remarks. "This is an amazing scene," he said to us. "You are helping to start a Christian revolution in this country, turning the thoughts of our government toward God. You are like a stone on the waters, and the ripples you stir up here will make it easier for others to follow." He then introduced General Nikolai Stolyarov, a KGB vice chairman in charge of all personnel.

We nodded in gratitude, but not without doubts in that setting. What impact can a stone have on a frozen lake? In his introductory statement, General Stolyarov did his best to dispel our doubts. A young, handsome man with a strong-boned face, Stolyarov had emerged as a popular hero during the August 1991 coup. A career officer in the Air Force, he had, at the height of the tension, flown to Gorbachev's *dacha* to help rescue him. The KGB job was his "reward."

Stolyarov began with an image obviously chosen for his religious audience, one that jarred us coming from a senior KGB official. "When the coup took place, it was as if the body of Christ had been taken, then resurrected. Our president was dead, and then alive again. I felt as if I had traveled all my life in the direction of that one moment. I was amazed at the peace I found at the moment of crisis, and amazed that I did not even have to use the gun at my side at such a time."

He went on for a few moments, detailing his actions against the coup. "Meeting with you here tonight," he concluded, "is a plot twist that could not have been conceived by the wildest fiction writer." Indeed. Stolyarov then opened the floor for questions.

What was his attitude toward Christians and Christian work? someone asked. "How to bring peace and quiet to the hearts of people is a great problem for us," the general replied. We are united with you in working together against the powers of evil." A few looks were exchanged around the room, and eyebrows arched upward. I thought cynically of the cockroaches in Sakharov's envelopes and the humiliating strip-search of Solzhenitsyn in the prison below.

Stolyarov continued, "We here in the USSR realize that too often we've been negligent in accepting those of the Christian faith. August 1991 shows what can happen. Seventy-four years ago we started with destruction, and now we are ending with destruction. Over the years we have destroyed many things of value. Now we have the problem: What to do next? The work of the KGB is familiar to you, of course, but now we have stopped our former existence. We are reorganizing. We have given some of our former authority to others."

He proceeded along this line, following a script that could have been written by Solzhenitsyn himself. "It is our capacity for repentance, not thinking, that differentiates us from the rest of animal creation," said Solzhenitsyn, and that is the improbable word Stolyarov turned to. "Political questions cannot be decided until there is sincere *repentance*, a return to faith by the people. That is the cross I must bear. I have been a member of the Party for twenty years. In our study of scientific atheism, we were taught that religion divides people. Now we see the opposite: love for God can only unite. Somehow we must learn to put together the missionary role—absolutely critical for us now—and also learn from Marx that man can't appreciate life if he is hungry."

Suddenly our heads were spinning. Was that "missionary role" he said? Where did he learn the phrase "bear a cross"? And the other word . . . *repentance*? Did the translator get that right? What to make of this never-never land in which the KGB now sounds like a seminarian? I glanced at Peter and Anita Deyneka, banned from the country for thirteen years, their visas always rejected because of their Christian activity, now munching cookies in the KGB headquarters. Hearing Stolyarov's words in the original Russian, and then in the English translation, they still could hardly believe them.

Stolyarov could not get off the hook so easily. Joel Nederhood, a refined, gentle man who makes radio and television broadcasts for the Christian Reformed Church, stood with a question. "General, many of us have read Solzhenitsyn's report of the gulag. A few of us have even lost family members there." His boldness caught some of his colleagues off guard, and the tension in the room noticeably thickened. "Your agency, of course, is responsible for overseeing the prisons. How do you respond to that past, and what changes have you put in place now?"

"I have spoken of repentance," Stolyarov replied in measured tones. "This is an essential step. You probably know of Abuladze's film by that title. There can be no *perestroika* apart from repentance. The time has come to repent of that past. We have broken the Ten Commandments, and for this we pay today."

I had seen *Repentance* by Tengiz Abuladze, and Stolyarov's allusion to it was no less startling than if he had cited Joseph McCarthy. The movie depicts false denunciations, forced imprisonment, the razing of churches—the very acts that had earned the KGB its reputation for cruelty in general and persecution of religion in particular. In Stalin's era an estimated 42,000 priests lost their lives. Ninety-eight of every one hundred Orthodox churches were shuttered. *Repentance* portrays these atrocities from the vantage point of one provincial town.

In the film's most tender scene, women of the village rummage through the mud of a lumberyard inspecting a shipment of logs that has just floated down the river. They are searching for messages from their imprisoned husbands who cut these logs in a labor camp. One woman finds initials carved into the bark and, weeping, caresses the log lovingly; it is a thread of connection to a husband she cannot caress. The movie ends with a peasant woman asking directions to a church. Told that she is on the wrong street, she replies, "What good is a street that doesn't lead to a church?"

Now, sitting in the state headquarters of tyranny, in a room built just above the Lubyanka interrogation rooms, we were being told something very similar by the vice chairman of the KGB. What good is a path that doesn't lead to repentance, to the Ten Commandments, to a church?

Someone asked Stolyarov about the KGB's close relationship with the Orthodox Church. He acknowledged the problem immediately, admitting his organization had used priests as informers and had planted their own personnel in key positions. "Our government too often ended up abusing the constitution rather than protecting it," he said. "I am cutting out these activities right away."

Without warning, the meeting took a more personal

turn. John Aker stood up. "General Stolyarov, I am a pastor from Rockford, Illinois. I began a career as an Army officer, and was trained as an Army Intelligence Agent. I taught courses in Soviet Bloc propaganda, and participated in two high-level counter-espionage activities that involved KGB officers.

"I grew up as a young boy in America very much afraid of the Soviet Union. That fear turned into distrust and finally, as an Army officer, it turned into hate.

"General, I feel very privileged to be here tonight. You said something that touched a chord deep within me. I have one thing to add, though. You used the phrase, 'That is the cross I must bear.' I went through a time when guilt over what I had done as an Army Intelligence Agent was destroying me. I couldn't bear that guilt, and I seriously considered ending my life. That's when I realized I did not have to bear that cross forever. Jesus bore it for me.

"Jesus' love for me has in turn given me a love for the people of the Soviet Union. This is my fourth visit in six months, and I have found them to be loving, kind, and searching people. General, I mean it sincerely when I say that as I think of you, I will pray for you."

John Aker sat down, and General Stolyarov gave a brief response. "I am deeply touched by your words. They coincide with my own feelings, too. In coming to this position—even here right now with the KGB—I determined that I would never use force in dealing with people. With every power that is in me, I wish to turn the position into good."

Next, Alex Leonovich spoke. Alex had been sitting at the head table translating for Stolyarov. Of all the representatives selected for our delegation, Alex had the deepest personal investment in the outcome. A native of Byelorussia, he had escaped Stalin's reign of terror as a boy of seven, emigrating to the United States. After our week in Moscow he would remain behind, in hopes of returning to the town of his birth for the first time in sixty-two years.

For forty-six of those years Alex had been broadcasting Christian radio programs, often jammed, back to his homeland. He knew personally many Christians who had been tortured and persecuted for their faith. They wrote to him faithfully when his programs got through. For him, to be sitting next to a high official of the KGB translating such a message of reconciliation was both bewildering and nearly incomprehensible.

Alex is a stout, grandfatherly bear of a man with gray hair and a look of kindness imprinted in the wrinkles of his face. He epitomizes the old guard of warriors who have prayed, sometimes believing and sometimes not, for more than half a century that change might come to the Soviet Union—the very change we apparently now were witnessing. He spoke slowly and softly in Russian to General Stolyarov, and the Russian speakers scattered around the room translated quietly for the rest of us.

"General, many members of my family suffered because of this organization," Alex said. "I myself had to leave the land that I loved. My uncle, who was very dear to me, went to a labor camp in Siberia and never returned. I cannot possibly tell you what it means to me to hear these words tonight. My heart is full.

"General, you say that you repent. Christ taught us how to respond. On behalf of my family, on behalf of my uncle who died in the gulag, I want you to know that in the spirit of Christ I forgive you." And then Alex Leonovich, evangelist and president of Slavic Missionary Service, reached over to General Nikolai Stolyarov, vice chairman of the KGB, and the two embraced in a Russian bear-hug.

Stolyarov whispered something to Alex, and not until later did we learn what he said. "Only two times in my life have I cried. Once was when I buried my mother. The other is tonight."

What was there left to do but pray? Our spokesman Mikhail Morgulis, a half-Jewish emigré whom Alex had befriended in New York and converted to Christ, rose to his feet and we all joined him. He prayed eloquently for "the thousands of our brothers and sisters who have perished," and for "the new leaders who would attempt to lead this nation down a new path." The television cameras clicked on, and cameramen vied for the best angle: Morgulis praying beneath the photo of Dzerzhinsky, the KGB guards peeking nervously about the room, General Stolyarov wiping awkwardly at his face.

After the prayer, our delegation presented Stolyarov with a Bible, a children's Bible, and a translation of the works of C. S. Lewis. "I feel like Moses," Alex said on the bus home that evening. "I have seen the promised land. I am ready for glory." He chided himself for his lack of faith. To him, and to others, our visit with the KGB seemed a sacred moment distilled from the prayers of an entire generation and poured out of a crucible of suffering.

The local photographer accompanying us had a less sanguine view. "It was all an act," he said. "They were putting on a mask for you. I can't believe it." But he too wavered, apologizing a few minutes later: "Maybe I was wrong. Maybe they have changed. I don't know what to believe anymore."

The next day's *Izvestiya*, a newspaper with a circulation of eight million, featured a story with the headline "First prayer at Lubyanka." Our visit, the article said, coincided with the official day designated for the memory of those who died in the labor camps. We listened to a translation of the glowing report on our visit, and afterward one member of our group made a poignant correction. "They got all the facts right but one. There have been many prayers at Lubyanka—down in the basement. This was merely the first to make the official record."

There is nothing as bitter as this moment when you go out to the morning roll call—in the dark, in the cold, with a hungry belly, to face a whole day of work. You lose your tongue. You lose all desire to speak to anyone.

— Alexander Solzhenitsyn,
One Day in the Life of Ivan Denisovich

CHAPTER FIVE

Basil and the Journalists

Each day, as members of our delegation assembled for planning and prayer, we tried to assimilate the swirl of change we were witnessing. Can it happen? Can not just a person but an entire nation change? Can the KGB reform? Before long, skepticism melted away. What transpired at the KGB headquarters was but one dramatic episode in a week that convinced us attitudes toward religion have undergone a seismic change in the former Soviet empire.

Almost overnight the nation has moved away from an official position of atheism and hostility to become perhaps the most open mission field in the world. Wherever we went, officials invited us to set up relief work, exchange programs, study centers, and religious publishing ventures. We heard reports that Young Life was inheriting camps from the Young Communists, and that the Gideons frantically were trying to resupply Bibles to hotel rooms (guests kept stealing them). Twenty-five hundred Soviet radio stations were carrying James Dobson's "Focus on the Family" program—more than in the United States, Canada, and the rest of the world combined. Campus Crusade staff members were preparing a curriculum on Christianity for the public schools.

After listening to a parade of politicians and government leaders express admiration and respect for Christianity, it was easy to lose sight of how radically the nation had changed. Soviet leaders seemed far more receptive to Christian influence than, say, their counterparts in the United States. Could their predecessors have been so devilish? An unexpected visit from Basil brought a jarring reminder of what life had been like for Christians under the Communist regime.

For years Basil, who lived in Moldavia, had clandestinely tuned in to short-wave programs by Alex Leonovich and Mikhail Morgulis. He had even heard Alex speak in person once, and ever since had harbored a desire to meet Alex again. Basil first heard a news item about Project Christian Bridge on "Voice of America." Then, incredulous, he listened as the national radio network gave reports of our meetings with the Supreme Soviet and the KGB. The new openness toward religion seemed so inconceivable to Basil that he got on a night train and made the fourteen-hour journey from Moldavia to Moscow in order to see us.

Somehow Basil found out what hotel we were

staying in. "It's the Oktyabrskaya—the one that used to belong to the Central Committee," he was told, and again he could hardly believe it. He showed up in the lobby early one morning, just as we were gathering to pray and to review the day's schedule.

Ron Nikkel of Prison Fellowship later said he could tell Basil had been a prisoner as soon as he walked into the room, because he stared down at the floor and avoided direct eye contact. Basil had broad, hulking shoulders and the rugged, weather-beaten features of a farmer. He looked ill at ease in a suit and tie.

Basil's smile was most peculiar: two front teeth on the top row were missing, and when he smiled gold fillings in the back molars gleamed faintly through the gap. He presented us with sacks of gorgeous purple grapes and golden apples, which he had hand-picked and carried on his lap from Moldavia. He asked for five minutes to address us.

When Basil opened his mouth and the first sound came out, I jumped. We were meeting in a small room, and Basil spoke at the decibel level of a freight train. I have never heard a louder voice from any human being. We soon learned why.

In 1962 Basil founded a small publishing company with his own funds. He printed gospel tracts, distributing a total of 700,000 before the KGB paid him a visit. They demanded that he stop, and when he refused they arrested him and sent him to a labor camp. At first Basil was perplexed. Why should he be punished for serving God? What use could he be in a labor camp? But then one morning he saw in a flash that God had provided a new opportunity.

Every morning before sunup prisoners from the labor camp had to assemble in an open space for roll call. Camp commanders insisted on strict punctuality from prisoners, but not from guards, and so thousands of prisoners stood outdoors several minutes each morning with nothing to do. Basil, who loved to preach, decided to start a church.

As he was recounting this story in the hotel room, Basil spoke louder and faster, gesturing passionately with his arms like an opera singer. Every few sentences the translator, Alex, grabbed Basil's flailing arm and asked him to please slow down and lower his voice. Each time Basil apologized, looked down at the floor, and began again in a pianissimo that within three seconds crescendoed to a fortissimo. His voice had no volume control, and the reason traced back to that early morning scene in the labor camp.

Basil preached daily to a truly captive audience. Typically, he had about two minutes before the guards arrived, rarely as long as five minutes, and as a result it took up to two weeks to deliver a single sermon. He had to shout to be heard by several thousand prisoners, a strain that made him hoarse until his voice adapted. Over the years—ten years in all—of preaching outdoors to thousands, he developed the habit of speaking at top volume and breakneck speed, a habit he could never break.

Basil completed his prison sentence in 1972 and devoted his energies to building an unregistered church in his village. Sometimes he visited the church among the convicts and, he proudly reported, even today a community of one hundred believers still worships in that labor camp.

Basil's difficulties did not end with his release from prison, though. He told us of harassment by the authorities over his unregistered church, of the threats and public slanders and repeated vandalism of the church building. Finally, after nineteen years, opposition had faded away and he had just laid the last cement block and covered the church with a roof. He had come to Moscow, he said, to thank us for all we were doing, to bring us fresh fruit from Moldavia, and to ask Alex Leonovich to speak at the dedication of his church.

"There were many years when I had no encouragement," Basil said. By now he was weeping openly and his voice cracked but did not drop one decibel. "The words of this man, Brother Leonovich, I carried in my heart. He was the one who encouraged me when my hands were tied behind my back." Basil then reached over, grabbed Alex by the shoulders, and kissed him in the Russian style once, twice, fifteen times—one for each year, he said, that he had waited for Alex to return.

"And now, such changes, I can hardly believe them," Basil said in closing. "We have been through the valley of tears. When Billy Graham came in 1959 they let him appear on a balcony but not speak. To think that you are here in Moscow, the center of unbelief, able to talk and drink tea with the leaders of our country. It is a miracle! Brothers and sisters, be bold! With your wings you are lifting up children of the Lord. Where I come from the believers are praying for you at this minute. We believe your visit will help reach our country for God. May God bless you all."

Suddenly, I burned with shame. Here we were: nineteen evangelical professionals who made a comfortable living from our faith sitting in one of the most luxurious hotels in Moscow. What did we know about the kind of bedrock faith needed in this nation of people who had endured such suffering? What gave us the right to represent the Basils of the land before Mikhail Gorbachev and the Supreme Soviet, let alone the KGB?

We stood and prayed with Basil, and then he left. Later that day Alex Leonovich traded in his airplane ticket, incurring a huge penalty, in order to extend his stay. "How could I possibly turn down Basil's invitation?" he said. Our group went off to be feted in grand style with a banquet at the Ukrainian embassy, and we did not see Basil again until later in the evening.

I looked forward to the event scheduled for that

evening, a visit to the Journalists' Club. The inordinately polite reception we were receiving in Moscow was making me nervous. I knew that an entire atheistic state had not warmed to Christianity overnight, and I longed for a dialogue of true substance. I wanted us to be challenged with hard questions about what difference Christianity could make in a country coming apart at the seams. I thought I could count on cynical, hard-bitten journalists to render such a challenge.

I thought wrong. This is what happened at the Journalists' Club of Moscow. First we North American Christians, seated on a spotlighted stage in a small theater, introduced ourselves. Ron Nikkel, normally taciturn, was feeling rather expansive. "Winston Churchill said you can judge a society by its prisons," he began. "By that standard, both the USSR and the United States are tragedies. Our prisons are awful.

"I have been in prisons all over the world, and have talked to sociologists, behaviorists, and criminal justice experts. None of them know how to get prisoners to change. But we believe—and I have seen abundant proof—that Christ can transform a person from the inside out. Jesus, himself a prisoner, was executed, but he rose again. Now many prisoners are rising again, thanks to him."

Ron then mentioned a prisoner in India who had returned to jail scores of times over a twenty-one year span. The criminal simply could not break the cycle, until he found Christ. Puzzled by his absence in court, the local magistrate visited the man's home and asked what had happened. "For the first time in my life, someone forgave me," the ex-prisoner answered.

The room fell silent, and then these "cynical, hard-bitten journalists" did something I would not have predicted in a thousand years. They broke into loud, prolonged applause. These are the probing questions they tossed at Ron: "What is this forgiveness? How can we find it? How do you get to know God?" Later, one of the Soviet journalists told us his profession had a special affinity for prisoners, since many had served time themselves.

When his turn came, Kent Hill introduced himself as the director of the Institute on Religion and Democracy. Several journalists leaned forward attentively. "It is no accident that democracy thrives alongside religion," Kent said. "Democracy is built on principles of individal human dignity. Our own Declaration of Independence acknowledges some rights as 'inalienable'—they are 'endowed by their Creator.' This fact puts limits on the power that any political leader can seize." Again the journalists applauded. Their follow-up comments showed that for them any connection between religion and democracy was an altogether novel idea.

Evidently, the journalistic elite of Moscow would not be the ones to challenge our basic Christian beliefs. They seemed far more intent on grasping after them, as if grasping for rare secrets of life that had been concealed for seventy years. After all of us seated onstage had introduced ourselves, the journalists responded.

A distinguished-looking, silver-haired gentleman stood first, identifying himself as an editor of the *Literary Gazette*, which we knew to be one of the most prestigious journals in the Soviet Union. "No doubt you know of the problems in our country," he said. "I tell you, however, that the greatest problem is not that we don't have enough sausages. Far worse, we don't have enough ideas. We don't know what to think. The ground has been pulled out from under us. We thank you deeply for coming to our country and holding before us morality, and hope, and faith. It is beautiful to see you in this place. You represent exactly what we need."

The next speaker was his polar opposite, a dissident who specialized in writing political satire. Slovenly dressed, ungroomed and passionate, with a bald head but spectacular two-inch eyebrows, he looked as if he had stepped straight from a Dostoyevsky novel. This character spoke in a voice almost as loud as Basil's. He had a bad stutter—odd to hear in a foreign language—and just as he reached a climactic point he would hang up on a word. "You are our salvation, our only hope!" he shouted. "We had a lawful country, a society with religious beliefs, but that was all destroyed in seventy years. Our souls were su-su-su-sucked out. Truth was de-de-destroyed. In the last stage, which we have just lived through, even the C-C-C-C-C-Communist morale was destroyed."

When a young journalist stood and headed for the exit, this firebrand turned on him in a fury, calling him down publicly. Finally, the emcee had to intervene and silence the stormy dissident. "I think our friend just went out for a smoke," he said. "Does someone else have a comment?"

A beautiful blonde woman wearing a red silk blouse and a leather skirt and matching boots made her way to the aisle. She stood just before the stage, her hands clutching a designer purse. I had not seen such fine clothes in Moscow. Mikhail Morgulis whispered to me that she was a popular newscaster, something like the Connie Chung of Russia. "I am so shaken to be here tonight," she said, and then paused a moment to control her voice.

"I am shaking! I feel so blessed to learn that American leaders are concerned with spiritual and moral problems. I am a person educated in religion and yet I am only on the first step in understanding what is God. So many visitors have come here to make a profit in our country, but I am so thankful that the American *intelligentsia* care enough to come and meet with people at such important levels over these issues."

She was followed by others who rose to give a similarly embarrassing overassessment of our importance as a delegation. As in previous meetings, we tried to mention flaws in American society and in the American church, but the journalists seemed altogether disinterested in apologies or critiques. They seemed, rather, starved—grievously starved for hope.

I thought of the reception our group might get at the Press Club in Washington, D.C., the questions we might prompt from the editors of *The New Republic* or *Esquire*. I tried to imagine Connie Chung or Barbara Walters being vulnerable before her peers, as this woman journalist had been. As I was mulling over these thoughts, I noticed in the audience a familiar figure in a funny green suit.

The theater lights had been dimmed for our introductions, but now that the audience was responding other lights were switched on. Sitting in the back row was Basil, he of the foghorn voice and the two-minute church in the gulag. From then on I kept one eye on Basil, wondering how an ex-convict from Moldavia felt in such an environment among the celebrities of Moscow.

Whenever someone mentioned the word "God" or "Jesus," Basil raised both fists over his head, and even from the stage I could almost see the gleam in the gap between his teeth. On the back row, out of view of the audience, Basil was acting as our one-person charismatic cheerleading crew.

For the first time that day I glimpsed our group as Basil saw us: his ambassadors, going where he would not be invited, speaking words he could not always follow, opening doors he had thought sealed shut forever. We, too, those of us who felt so unworthy in his presence that morning, had a role to play.

Basil stood for millions of Christians who had lived out their faith in fear and trembling. Incredibly, the tables had turned. Now the journalists of Moscow applauded when they heard stories of converted prisoners, and craved news about God as a dying patient craves a miracle cure. They hung on our words about Christianity as Russian economists hung on words about capitalism, as if we were smuggling in a secret formula from the West that might salvage their land.

We were not bringing imports from the West, however. The God we served had been in Russia all along, worshiped hungrily in the camps and in the unregistered house churches and in the cathedrals the Communists had not razed.

These journalists, all masters of Moscow's cocktail party circuit, had never met a simple saint like Basil. It was our job, quite simply, to introduce them.

All that the downtrodden can do is go on hoping. After every disappointment they must find fresh reason for hope.
— *Alexander Solzhenitsyn,*
The Gulag Archipelago

CHAPTER SIX
Interlude in Zagorsk

We had one Sunday on our own in Moscow and our delegation scattered to different churches. Partly because of comments by the journalists, I wanted to attend a Russian Orthodox service.

In almost every meeting with our Soviet hosts, questions about the church had surfaced. No one questioned the need for religion, but everyone questioned the kind of religion. What did we think of the Russian Orthodox? Did we intend to cooperate with them? Did we think the Russian Orthodox capable of leading a national moral reform?

The wording of some of these questions betrayed the askers' suspicions. Some thought a history of coziness with the Communist party had fatally compromised the powerful Russian Orthodox Church. One government minister put it bluntly: "The Orthodox Church has taken over the very worst aspects of communism."

The persistent questions led to some heated discussion within the ranks of our delegation. Those who had many years of experience working in the USSR tended to disparage the Russian Orthodox Church. "No group is more *opposed* to what we hope to accomplish," said one veteran. He had seen the church comply with the persecution of unregistered believers, and had watched with dismay as church officials mouthed the Party line at world religious gatherings.

Furthermore, what made us think the Russian Orthodox would be open to cooperation with evangelical groups? During our week in Moscow, the Church Patriarch refused to grant an audience to Pope John Paul II, who wished to visit Moscow, on account of the Catholics' penchant for proselytism. What would he think of the evangelical missionary movement?

In the end, though, our group agreed to avoid all criticism of the Russian Orthodox Church. We would identify ourselves as Protestant evangelicals, and stress our emphasis on the Bible. If questioned further we would reply that it is essential for all Christians— Catholics, Protestants, and Orthodox—to work together in meeting the country's spiritual needs. This decision seemed vindicated when the Patriarch, in all his pomp and ceremony, paid an official visit to the Russian Bible Society to mark its re-opening. As a sponsoring partner, the Orthodox denomination had thrown its full weight behind the Bible Society.

Within our group Ron Nikkel, president of Prison Fellowship International, spoke most emphatically for cooperation. "The priests already have the respect of the people," he insisted. (Polls show that Soviets are eight times more likely to trust a religious leader than a political leader.) "They have resources, the loyalty of fifty million members, and a long tradition of spiritual authority. We must not try to work against them."

Ron said he had met many priests who demonstrated a deep spirituality and a genuine compassion for the people. When I asked to see an example of this compassion at work, Ron arranged a trip fifty miles northeast from Moscow to visit two sites: the Zagorsk Monastery, richest jewel of the Russian Orthodox Church, and the Zagorsk prison, possibly the worst prison in the country.

Ron and I stepped out of the hotel on a cold Sunday morning to look for Sasha's aging, clattery sedan of Russian make. Sasha, an engineer with a social conscience, had begun visiting the Zagorsk prison two years before, making the long drive once a week. Initially he had only disdain for the Russian Orthodox Church, but encounters with the monks at Zagorsk changed his outlook, and recently Sasha had begun attending an Orthodox church in downtown Moscow.

Sasha was a thin, small man, with a long, pointed beard that any Russian priest might envy. A fitness buff, he went for a five-mile run every morning, followed by an invigorating swim in the Moscow River (except in deepest winter, when the ice grew too thick to chop through by hand). He had arisen at 5:00 A.M. that morning in order to complete his regimen.

Sasha understood English, but spoke little. For help with translation he had brought along his sixteen-year-old daughter Julia, a pretty, dark-haired girl with an athlete's build. I learned she was the second-ranked girl's tennis player in Moscow, and was hoping to win a scholarship from a college in Alabama. "Well, you see, I don't have so many clever brains," Julia said, apologizing for her obsession with sports. Her brains proved sufficiently clever to get us through some difficult translation.

We drove through Moscow along the river boulevard that runs beside the Kremlin complex. It was a startlingly clear day, temperature in the low twenties, and the gold onion domes of the Kremlin cathedrals, glittering with ice crystals, shone like miniature suns against a deep blue sky. The river was blackened silver. In Red Square, long lines were already forming by Lenin's tomb and the fairy-tale spires of St. Basil's Cathedral. Sasha pulled to the curb to allow us to take in the view, one of the most breathtaking man-made sights in the world.

Drab gray suburbs outside Moscow soon yielded to rolling hills and birch forests. A light dusting of snow from the previous night gave the scenery a postcard-like quality. Among the trees we saw a few farmhouses from tsarist times, their decorative woodwork restored and painted with bright colors. After an hour of driving we came over a rise and there, spread out before us, was the monastery of Zagorsk.

Zagorsk is a feast for the eyes, a veritable Disneyland of sacred architecture. A cluster of fifty magnificent buildings that includes two cathedrals, numerous chapels, a tsar's palace, and a wood-frame hospital, the monastery showcases the finest architectural styles from the fifteenth to the seventeenth century. The largest cathedral was built by an Italian in Renaissance style. The most enchanting, Moorish in appearance, has four symmetrical blue domes that shimmer with inlaid gold stars. Monks keep the monastery grounds in spotless condition, and tree-lined walks lead from one architectural treasure to another. Zagorsk sheltered the last enclave of

Russian civilization in the days of the Tatar invaders, and had long served as seat of the Russian Patriarch, the Pope of the East.

Brother Bonifato, a red-bearded priest dressed in flowing black robes, met our car at the gate and ushered us into the rococo Cathedral of the Assumption, where a service was underway. Ducking in a private side-entrance, we immediately found ourselves on the front row of a small, vaulted chapel attached to the main cathedral. Before us loomed a wall that appeared covered with solid gold, inset with the five-tiered iconostasis. Ensconced candles lent a soft, eerie glow to the room, as if the walls were the source, rather than reflection, of light.

We stood beside a 150-voice choir composed entirely of young monks in training. (Zagorsk turns away three to four applicants for every candidate it admits.) The air hummed with the throaty, bass-clef harmony of the Russian liturgy, a sound that seemed to come from under the floor. After the choir had sung a few bars, they were answered antiphonally by a choir of equal size, hidden from view in another chapel.

The vaulting caused sound waves to bounce down on us again and again in harmonic overtones, creating an intense aural effect. That, combined with the scent of melting candle wax and burning incense, made for a very sensuous service. I could easily understand the sentiments of Prince Vladimir's emissaries who had first recommended converting Russia's tribes to Christianity. Hearing this same liturgy on a visit to Constantinople, they reported back, "We knew not whether we were in heaven or on earth, for on earth there is no such splendor or such beauty."

The service seemed very Old Testament in style. Ancient Hebrews had no icons, of course, but Russian believers treated the iconostasis almost like an altar, lighting candles before it and using the icons as a focal point for meditation and supplication. As in the Old Testament, only priests were allowed behind the high altar where the elements were prepared. Periodically, priests wearing bejeweled robes and elaborate head-dresses swept up and down the aisle in a glittering procession, swinging incense containers or holding up a Bible encased within a gold cover studded with precious stones.

An Orthodox service lasts three to four hours, with worshipers entering and leaving at will. The audience has little participation; a concept like "the priesthood of all believers" is utterly foreign. No one invites congregants to "pass the peace" or "greet the folks around you with a smile." They stand—there are no chairs or pews—and watch the professionals, who are very professional indeed. I caught a glimpse of the main cathedral area, packed with over two thousand worshipers, many of them younger than thirty.

The service had undeniable power, and it gave me an understanding of both the praise and criticism I had heard regarding the Orthodox Church. Admirers commended its spirit of reverence and worship. By carrying on a ritual virtually unchanged in a millennium, the church had given the Russian people a sense of stability and permanence unavailable elsewhere in their turbulent society. It had preserved the message of the gospel by enfolding it in pictures, songs, and imagery that any illiterate peasant could comprehend.

Critics, on the other hand, pointed out the irrelevance of the church. By adhering to a form based on liturgy dispensed by distant professionals, the church was perpetuating the vast societal gulf that had always divided Russia. People had no model of how to apply Christianity to daily life. Dostoyevsky made this complaint forcefully in *The Brothers Karamazov*. The church relies on "miracle, mystery, and authority," said the Grand Inquisitor: the three temptations rejected by Christ in the wilderness, but adopted by the church ever since.

Bonifato, however, as well as Nikodim and several other brothers from the Zagorsk Monastery, were breaking the stereotypes of the Church of Irrelevance. From that sublime service Brother Bonifato led us straight to one of bleakest settings imaginable. "Really, it's a dungeon," Ron Nikkel warned as we traveled a mile to the Zagorsk prison. "Like you'd expect to find in Dickens's day. I haven't seen such conditions outside of Africa." Aware that Ron had toured prisons in fifty different countries, I braced myself for the worst.

I found the worst. Zagorsk prison, oldest in Russia, was constructed in 1832, and the builders set its stone walls below ground to cut down the need for heating. To reach the prisoners' quarters, we went through four steel gates, down, down, down worn stone steps that led progressively toward the source of an acrid stench, the prisoners' cells on the bottom level.

The first cell we entered was ten feet by twelve feet, about the size of my bedroom in Chicago. Eight teenage boys—the youngest was actually twelve—jumped to attention when the door opened. The room held only four beds, so two boys slept on each bed. There was a rickety table, but no other furniture. Each boy had a plastic bag hanging from the end of his bed that contained one change of clothing, the only belongings permitted. A thin, soiled blanket covered each bed, but I saw no sheets or pillowcases.

In one corner of the room was a ceramic-lined hole in the ground with two footpads marked out for squatting. This hole, open to view on all sides, functioned as both toilet and "shower," although the only water came from a cold water spigot an arm's length away. The basement cell had a single six-inch window, frosted over and welded shut, at the very top of one wall. A bare bulb dangled at the end of a wire descending from the ceiling.

There were no board games, no television or radio sets, no diversions of any kind. All day every day for a year, two years, maybe five, these boys had nothing to do but lie on their beds or pace around the room, waiting for freedom. Most of them, I learned, were serving time for petty theft.

The room had one bright spot of color: a crude, arched altar fashioned out of tinfoil adorned one wall, home for some tiny painted icons that Brother Nikodim had donated. He had also given the boys a supply of Christian books. Brother Bonifato introduced us to each youngster, moving easily among them, resting his hand on their shoulders as he talked.

The women's quarters were even worse. They lived four to a cell in a room half the size. Bunks sticking out from the wall left an aisle barely wide enough to stand in. The women had no special amenities; their toilet and "shower" arrangements were exactly the same as the men's.

When the steel door to one women's cell opened I could hardly see inside, the room was so thick with what looked like fog. We soon saw why. One of the women had rigged up a crude electrical contraption: by twisting a lamp cord wire around a live wire near the ceiling, she had managed to divert an electrical current. The lamp cord, crudely spliced in three places, fed current to a rusty electrical coil, which was heating water in a small tin basin. From the looks of the fog, the women kept the water boiling all day: it provided some heat for their stone-walled cell, and gave a source of hot water for bathing as well. Did they also make coffee out of that rusty brown water? I flinched at the thought.

For security purposes, Zagorsk observes a permanent twenty-four-hour lockdown. Prisoners don't take walks in the hallway, visit a cafeteria, or go outdoors to an exercise yard. Male and female, young and old, they sit in their tiny dungeon cells like animals, interrupted only by the food that comes once a day. They cannot even see into the hallway. A solid steel door seals off every cell, except for a tiny hinged grate that a guard can pull back to peer inside.

Yet when the prisoners spoke of their main worry, it concerned life outside the prison, not inside. Russia has always maintained a strict policy against hiring ex-convicts. As the law now stands, upon release, these prisoners will get a "convicted" stamp on their identity cards, which will make them ineligible for employment. Few have families to support them; without income, what alternative do they have to stealing food or supplies and landing back in prison?

The warden turned out to be a dedicated, even courageous man. In a country fast disintegrating, prison budgets get cut first. Two years before, when the government shut off his supplies of food, this warden approached the monks at the monastery for help. Out of their own storehouses, the monks donated enough bread and vegetables to feed the prisoners throughout the winter.

The monks' selfless response impressed the warden, a Communist at the time. "I don't know where the country will go in the future," he told us. "Right now with all the changes in the KGB I don't even know who my boss is. Who can I write with my requests for aid? As for this place, we are turning back to our ancient roots in the church. Where else can we turn?"

The warden spoke candidly as we met in his office after our tour. He was responsible for six hundred prisoners and his dispensary contained not a single aspirin. He asked Ron for help in procuring antibiotics, bandages, and basic medical supplies.

Ron described a prison in Brazil run by Christians associated with Prison Fellowship, and the warden listened intently. He volunteered to go to Brazil and look it over, then report back to his superiors—after he found out who they were. The two discussed the possibility of Prison Fellowship assuming management of the worst prison in Russia to use it as a model of reform.

On his own, the warden had already asked the monks about moving some of the prisoners to one of the properties the government had recently returned to the church. Trusted prisoners could live there, do the work of restoration free of charge, and raise crops to feed their fellow prisoners back in Zagorsk.

In 1989 the warden had authorized the monks to rebuild a chapel in the prison basement—an act of remarkable boldness for a Communist functionary in the atheistic state prevailing then. Just before leaving Zagorsk prison, Ron and I asked if we could see the result of their work.

Located on the lowest subterranean level, the chapel was an oasis of beauty in an otherwise grim dungeon. The priests had installed a marble floor, and mounted finely wrought candle sconces on the walls. Prisoners spent many hours cleaning out a seventy-year accumulation of filth from the room, which had been used as a storeroom. They took pride in their chapel, the only prison chapel, we were told, in all of Russia. Each week priests traveled from the monastery to conduct a service there, and for this occasion prisoners were allowed out of their cells, which naturally guaranteed excellent attendance.

We spent a few minutes admiring the handiwork that went into the room, and Brother Bonifato mentioned that the icon for the prison chapel was "Our Lady Who Takes Away Sadness." Ron commented that there must be much sadness within these walls, then turned to Brother Bonifato and asked if he would say a prayer for the prisoners. Brother Bonifato looked puzzled, and Ron repeated, "Could you say a prayer for the prisoners?"

"A prayer? You want a prayer?" Brother Bonifato asked, and we nodded. He looked thoughtful, then disappeared behind the altar at the end of the room. He brought out an icon of Our Lady Who Takes Away Sadness, which he propped up on a stand. Then he retrieved two candle holders and two incense bowls, which he laboriously hung in place and lit.

Ron and I looked at each other and rolled our eyes. We were already an hour late for a meeting back in Moscow. "Sorry," Ron whispered, "I guess extemporaneous prayer isn't in his repertoire."

Brother Bonifato was far from finished. He removed his headpiece and outer vestments. He meticulously laced gold cuffs over his black sleeves. He placed a droopy gold stole around his neck, and then a gold crucifix. He carefully fitted a different, more formal headpiece on his head. Before each action, he paused to kiss the cross or genuflect. Finally, he was ready to pray.

Prayer involved a new series of formalities. Brother Bonifato did not say prayers; he sang them, from a liturgy book propped on another stand. At one point he paused to teach us a few Russian sentences so we could join in. Finally, twenty minutes after Ron had requested a prayer for the prisoners, Brother Bonifato said, "Amen," and we exited the prison into the wonderful fresh air outside.

The procedure in the prison chapel brought back for me the inner conflict I had felt while worshiping in the monastery cathedral that morning. Reverence, submission, awe, *mysterium tremendum*—the Russian Orthodox Church knew these qualities well, and conveyed them superbly in worship. But God remained faraway, approachable only after much preparation and only through intermediaries such as priests and icons.

I thought of the teenagers back in their basement cell. If one of them needed prayer, for the strength to endure or for a sick family member outside, would Brother Bonifato have followed the same ritual? Would the boys in the cell dare to think of approaching God themselves, praying in the casual and everyday language that Jesus used?

Yet there is no Prison Fellowship staff person to assign to Zagorsk—not yet anyway—no paid chaplains, Young Life, or Youth for Christ volunteers to send into the dungeon. There is only the monastery of the Russian Orthodox Church, which next to the government remains the most powerful institution in Russia. When the need arose, the monks had responded: with bread, with their incarnational presence, with the re-institution of worship in the unlikeliest of places. I had seen the best and worst of Russia in one morning in Zagorsk, and for just a moment they had come together.

Left, above: **Konstantin Lubenchenko**, newly elected chairman of the Supreme Soviet, told us, "We need Bibles here very much. Is there a way to distribute them free of charge so more people can get them?"

Right: After a prayer, **Mikhail Morgulis** presented a Bible to **General Nikolai Stolyarov**, second in command of the KGB.

Left: "There were many years when I had no encouragement. And now, such changes, I can hardly believe them," **Basil** said in closing.

Below: **Alex Leonovich** epitomizes the old guard of warriors who have prayed for more than half a century that change might come to Russia.

Top: Zagorsk is a feast for the eyes, a veritable Disneyland of sacred architecture.

Center, left: "We are in a crisis, a spiritual crisis," **Mikhail Gorbachev** said. "... More than ever before, we need support from our partners, and I value solidarity with religion."

Top: After meeting with the delegation, **Gorbachev** shook hands with each member. Here he is greeting **Peter** and **Anita Deyneka**, while **Philip Yancey** and **John Van Diest** look on.

Above: Signs of awakening were everywhere. Vendors sold merchandise openly on Arbat Street. . . . Muscovites danced in the streets. How long will the dance last?

Do you know what astounds me most about the world? It is the impotence of force to establish anything. . . . In the end, the sword is always conquered by the mind.

— *Napoleon*

CHAPTER SEVEN

Man of the Decade

Dostoyevsky wrote, "A person cannot live without worshiping something." On the drive back into Moscow, I noted a striking similarity between the religions of Russia's distant past and its recent past. An elaborate mausoleum at Zagorsk displayed the preserved body of Father Sergy, a great patriot and Russian saint, and pilgrims had come from miles around to touch or kiss the coffin. Those lines formed a mirror image of the lines snaking out from Lenin's tomb in Red Square. The cathedral had rows of icons; the streets of Moscow had rows of statues. The Zagorsk prison had Our Lady Who Takes Away Sadness; the KGB headquarters had (until recently) a monument to its founder, who had given the nation so much sadness. The Communists had replaced a God-man with their own man-gods.

Those of us from a democratic tradition, accustomed to casual jokes about politicians, can hardly fathom the absolute power once wielded by Soviet leaders. Solzhenitsyn tells of a hapless workman who got ten years in prison for hanging his coat on a bust of Lenin, and of a woman who got ten years for carelessly scribbling a note on a newspaper over a picture of Stalin. Another scene recorded in *The Gulag Archipelago* shows the outer limits of the cult of personality. The speaker at an obscure district Party meeting called for a tribute to Comrade Stalin (who was not even present). All rose for the obligatory applause which rolled on and on, until suddenly it dawned upon the assembled Party members that someone must be the first to stop clapping. No one dared. Applause went on for five minutes, nine, ten, eleven minutes. At last the manager of a local paper factory, tired and sore-palmed, quit slapping his hands together. He was promptly arrested and served ten years for showing disrespect to the Great Leader.

Against this background of despotism that had characterized all but a few years of the Soviet regime, Mikhail S. Gorbachev brought a wholly new style. It took years for the Soviet people to trust the new words, *glasnost* and *perestroika*, that suddenly dominated their vocabulary. It took the West even longer to trust the olive branches Gorbachev held out. Would he really allow the Berlin Wall to come down? Was he serious about nuclear disarmament? Ultimately, Gorbachev won over most skeptics. He was awarded a Nobel Peace Prize and designated *Time* magazine's "Man of the Decade."

At the time of our visit, Gorbachev still retained the title President of the Soviet Union, but no one knew what power that office held or indeed how much longer the term "Soviet Union" would have any meaning. (During our week in Moscow the red, white, and blue Russian flag conspicuously appeared over Kremlin buildings, replacing the red Soviet flag.) Throughout the trip, our promised meeting with Gorbachev hung in limbo, subject to such exigencies as the latest political crisis, his sudden trip to Madrid for the Middle-East Peace Conference, the state of the economy. Our delegation hoped a meeting would take place, but we did not hear definite word until the Sunday night I returned from Zagorsk, a few days before our scheduled departure. By then we had received a good dose of Soviet cynicism about Gorbachev.

On Arbat Street the tourist trinket of choice was a "Gorby doll," a political take-off on the Russian *Matreshka* dolls. Traditional *Matreshka* dolls, hand-painted on wood, portray a chubby-faced child in exquisite Russian costume. The doll breaks apart at the stomach, and inside is an exact duplicate, only slightly smaller. That one also breaks apart, spilling out many identical dolls, each fitting snugly into the other, until at last the tiniest doll is uncovered. You see these dolls displayed everywhere in Moscow, their ten or eleven components lined up stair-step like a family of clones.

Gorby dolls vary the pattern. The smallest doll is a likeness of Marx, who is enclosed within Lenin, who is in turn swallowed up by Stalin, Khrushchev, and then Brezhnev. The largest doll will vary, depending on the artist's politics. Some feature Gorbachev on the outside, enclosing Yeltsin; some have Yeltsin enclosing Gorbachev. A few have Yeltsin's profile painted on the front of the largest doll and Gorbachev's on the back— "Twins, just alike," say the salesmen. The dolls communicate a less-than-subtle message: nothing much has changed. Faces may vary, but they're all Communists of one form or another.

That simmering political cynicism may, ironically, be one of the surest signs that democracy is taking hold at the grass roots. At the least, it shows the decline of the absolute dictator.

It was with a high level of anticipation that we retraced our steps to the Kremlin to meet with Gorbachev. By then we had become well-acquainted with "the Russian style." We would gather in the hotel lobby at the appointed time, stand around for an hour or so, call the bus company about the no-show bus, wait for a replacement (typically, the driver of the original bus would not call in when his vehicle broke down), then wind our way through Moscow streets to the appointed place. Every meeting started well behind schedule, and involved long, flowery introductions. Only after much ceremonious talk did the discussion settle down to matters of substance.

Gorbachev was different. Our bus was late, as usual, and when we motored through the red brick Spassky Gate, presidential assistants met us on the run, gesturing wildly for us to hurry. A procession of evangelicals dressed in our best suits sprinted across cobblestone plazas and alleyways until we reached the presidential office complex, in an elegant hall built by the tsars. Security guards with two-way radios directed us to leave our overcoats—surprisingly, we went through no metal detectors or body frisks—and thirty seconds later we were escorted in, breathing heavily, to meet Gorbachev.

He shook hands with each member of the delegation, motioned us to our seats, and began precisely at 11:00, as scheduled. A cortege of intense young men entered through a side door, bearing plates of biscuits and cups of tea served on state china. Clearly, Gorbachev had mastered the Western style of doing business. He gave an opening statement that showed he had been well briefed, and spoke right to the point, maintaining excellent eye contact the entire time.

"I have read your letter, and I thank you for it," he began.* "I found it very warm and moving. I do not get many such letters. Mostly I get letters from people who are worried. 'What is going to happen? Our country is in a difficult time,' they say. I share those worries. We are in a crisis, including a spiritual crisis, as the country undergoes so many changes so quickly.

"Civil strife and division are springing up everywhere. In the past change in my country has come with a circle of blood; now we are trying to bring about change democratically. If we succeed it will be good for all of us. But for the democratic process to work here, we will need a profound and systemic reform. Getting to that point is a very difficult challenge."

Gorbachev seemed vigorous and healthy. His skin looked tanned, thanks to the makeup he wore as a concession to the omnipresent cameras. He was fully in command.

"Let me be honest with you—I am an atheist," the president added, setting to rest all rumors about his being a closet believer. "I believe that man is at the center and must solve his own problems. That is my faith. Even so, I have profound respect for your beliefs. This time, more than ever before, we need support from our partners, and I value solidarity with religion. As you know, we have many important decisions to make, and this is a very busy day. The next hour, I am meeting with presidents of all the republics. But I felt it necessary to carve out this time with you. Raisa assured me it was important!"

At this point Lubenchenko, chairman of the Supreme Soviet, broke in. "But," he said with a wink, "if the president finds betrayal repugnant, shows compassion for his

* The letter stating the goals of Project Christian Bridge appears in Appendix A on page 91.

fellow man, encourages freedom, respects the decency and rights of individuals, and has the goal of moving toward the good, then perhaps words don't matter so much. Perhaps by deeds he is a believer, if not by words."

Gorbachev laughed. "I do not object. I must say that for a long time I have drawn comfort from the Bible. Ignoring religious experience has meant great losses for society. And, I must acknowledge that Christians are doing much better than our political leaders on the important questions facing us. We welcome your help, especially when it is accompanied by deeds. My favorite line in your letter is, 'Faith without deeds is dead.' "

Joel Nederhood and Mikhail Morgulis responded on our behalf, in this fashion: "Mr. President, we support you. We honor you for taking the time to meet with us, and also for the many changes you have brought to the world. You are in our prayers. We represent millions of Christians in North America who pray for you, and who have a long history of helping people in need. We will carry a message back to them, and do our best to direct aid to the Soviet Union—both spiritual and material aid. We believe the world is a safer and freer place because of you. We believe you have been chosen by God for your task."

At that last comment a delphic smile crossed Gorbachev's face. "I am deeply moved," he said. "We are learning, though, that in a democratic country we need support not only from God but from the people!" He added a few comments about the August coup, and the need for his nation to punish the coup plotters while avoiding undue revenge.

As the meeting proceeded, Gorbachev grew more and more relaxed. He departed from his prepared notes, and seemed to welcome a more casual discussion. Mikhail Morgulis, taking note of this change, ventured,

"Mr. President, perhaps this meeting itself is one of the best proofs of the existence of God. Christians have not always been so welcome in this room, and for more than a year I have been praying for this meeting to take place!" Gorbachev laughed and nodded approval. "Yes, yes, well, it has taken a long time, but it's important to have patience."

Gorbachev had promised us fifteen minutes and gave us almost forty. He stood respectfully as Morgulis led a brief prayer, posed for a few official photos, shook hands with us again, and hurried off to his luncheon with the presidents.

For some members of the group, the meeting with Gorbachev represented a high-water mark. More than any other event in the trip, it showed the profound change in the official attitude toward Christians. A few days before, a government minister had attended the reopening of the Russian Bible Society, an organization that had not been allowed to function for seventy years. "We have treated this book like a bomb," he said, holding up a Bible. "Like contraband material, we have not allowed Bibles into our country. Now we realize how wrong that was." Mikhail Gorbachev was in many ways personally responsible for the loosening of the bonds that had restricted the practice of religion.

And yet other members of the group expressed disappointment after the meeting—not with Gorbachev, but with us. For nearly a week we had been praying that we not be dazzled by the trappings of power. "How would Jesus conduct himself in the halls of the Kremlin?" one member had challenged us. We agreed to leave all cameras behind, to observe the strictest protocol, to present Mr. Gorbachev with a Bible and downplay all other gifts. But when the meeting took place, the aura of fame proved overwhelming. For hours afterward, the group basked in the glow of having sat in the presence of one of the great men of the century.

Later that afternoon Gorbachev's office called to report that he had been most impressed with the goals of Project Christian Bridge. "My meeting with the presidents could have used some of that harmony and good spirit!" Gorbachev remarked. He asked permission to release the text of our mission statement to the Associated Press, along with photos of our meeting. In a lead article about our visit to Moscow, the Soviet paper *Izvestiya* made perhaps the most appropriate observation, "Truly the ways of the Lord are inscrutable."

The struggle against religion is not a campaign, not an isolated phenomenon, not a self-contained entity; it is an inseparable component . . . an essential link and necessary element in the complex of Communist education.
— Pravda, January 12, 1967

If you meet with difficulties in your work, or suddenly doubt your abilities, think of him—of Stalin—and you will find the confidence you need. If you feel tired in an hour when you should not, think of him—of Stalin—and your work will go well. If you are seeking a correct decision, think of him—of Stalin—and you will find that decision.
— Pravda, February 17, 1950

CHAPTER EIGHT
Fall from Grace

As a journalist, I eagerly anticipated our scheduled meeting with the staff of *Pravda*. The Soviet Union had little tradition of free speech or free press—until recently all photocopy machines were kept locked, and one had to apply for permission to own a typewriter—and I wondered how *Pravda*, formerly the official mouthpiece of the Communist party, was coping with all the changes. President Gorbachev edged away from rigid Marxism after the Party betrayed him. But *Pravda* had brazenly supported the August coup. Shut down by Boris Yeltsin as punishment for that treachery, the paper had only recently resumed publication.

Pravda has a fabled history. Founded in 1912, it predates the Revolution, and enlarged photos in its office lobby show Lenin personally poring over typesetting galleys. Everyone knew the paper used to present as much propaganda as news. (Russians enjoyed this play on words about their two largest newspapers, *Pravda*, meaning "Truth," and *Izvestiya*, meaning "News": "There is no 'pravda' in *Izvestiya* and no 'izvestiya' in *Pravda*.") Still, reading *Pravda* was compulsory for any citizen of note. Many careers and even lives have been determined by a few sentences in *Pravda*.

The newspaper occupied a large, five-story building in the heart of Moscow's printing district, but many offices in that building now sat vacant. Numbers tell the dramatic story of *Pravda*'s fall from grace: daily circulation has plummeted from eleven million to 700,000. *Pravda* has cut four-fifths of its foreign correspondents and reduced its overall staff by two-thirds. It loses money on every subscription, and must scramble to obtain enough paper to stay in print.

The editor-in-chief, accompanied by several senior editors, met with us in a rather spare, functional conference room used mainly for editorial planning meetings. He spoke for about fifteen minutes, detailing the "challenges" facing his paper, and then turned the meeting over to a younger editor, a senior correspondent who would soon move to Washington and head up the U.S. bureau.

Like an optimistic surgeon discussing an AIDS patient, the editor-in-chief tried to put the best face on *Pravda*'s crisis even while admitting the prognosis looked grim. It soon became apparent why our delegation had been invited to these offices: we got the unsettling feeling of being used in a kind of reverse propaganda. The official organ of the Communist party, utterly discredited, was in an act of desperation reaching out to its antithesis—evangelical Christianity—as a way of gaining credibility, or at least gaining sales.

What about reprinting from the Bible? one of our group asked. Excellent idea, said the editors. We welcome reprints from your "holy books." How about a column on religion? Splendid! Can you suggest a writer?

The editors sought to rehabilitate *Pravda*'s image by taking the moral high ground. "The most important principle to us is reconciliation," they told us. "We strive to bring our people together. The past months have shown that our level of civilization is still low. We don't know how to settle disputes in a civilized, peaceful way. We must find a way to reform our people from the inside. We must learn to settle differences by civilized—one could even say Christian—means."

Conversation turned to the question of how one comes up with the moral principles worth advocating. Early Communists believed that they—not God—were the ones to determine morality, which could then be enforced from the top down. The history of communism proves beyond all doubt that goodness cannot be legislated from the Kremlin and enforced at the point of a gun. In a great irony, attempts to compel morality tend to produce rebellious subjects and tyrannical rulers.

As the quintessential propaganda vehicle *Pravda* had, after all, always taken a moral stance; the problem was that the moral principles shifted depending on who was in power. Currently *Pravda* was showing admirable compassion for the victims of the Chernobyl disaster; they gave us sample drawings by the children of Chernobyl which they were using as a fundraiser. But the same newspaper had, for example, shown no compassion whatever for the children victims of Stalin's enforced starvation of the Ukraine. What "higher law" determined when compassion applied and when it did not?

Pravda had no answer. The editors readily acknowledged that their nation was facing perhaps the greatest crisis in its history, and they agreed about the nature of that crisis. We cited what a prominent government economist had told us: "The worst crisis these days is morality. Ideology, which was a religion for us, has been crushed. Yet there is no Christ to replace it." These seemed to us surprising words from a businessman devoted to improving the material state of the country, but the *Pravda* editors concurred. "Yes, he's right. It's the worst crisis, worse than the economic and political problems."

Listening to the editors gathered around the table, I could easily sense their inner tumult. They had risen through the ranks because of their staunch loyalty to Marxist doctrine—some had still not renounced their Party membership—and yet they now knew the ideology had failed miserably. What could replace it? I thought of an ironic term from chemistry, "free radicals": these editors were looking for some particle of reality to attach themselves to.

Unaccountably, I found myself feeling something like pity for the editors. They were not the horned demons I had envisioned in high school. They were earnest, sincere, searching—and badly shaken. Shaken to the foundations. They clung, as if by their fingernails, to the original vision of justice and equality espoused by Marx and Lenin. Yet even while clinging, they admitted the pursuit of that vision had produced the worst nightmares the world has ever seen.

I tried to put myself in their place. I, too, am an editor committed to an ideology. I, too, have sat around a conference table and discussed the best way to present a vision of truth to my readers. What must it be like to get dressed every morning and come to work knowing that the vast majority of my former readers have repudiated everything I have always believed, but not knowing what else to believe?

Reflecting back on the meeting with *Pravda*, Martin DeHaan of the "Radio Bible Class" drew the direct analogy to us. "How would we evangelicals feel," he said, "if our Christian faith were exposed as a fraud—if we learned that Christ had not risen after all?" The apostle Paul toyed with that hypothetical question. "And if Christ has not been raised, our preaching is useless and so is your faith," he thundered in 1 Corinthians 15. "More than that, we are then found to be false witnesses . . . we are to be pitied more than all men." Down deep, at the core, all of us would be shattered. We would know that the center of our faith, that upon which we had built our lives and invested all our hopes, had been destroyed. A corpse cannot be the Lord of Creation.

I sensed in these Communist editors something like that upheaval. Early Communists had promised the emergence of a new breed of human being, the "New Socialist Man," who would demonstrate superior noble character. Leon Trotsky wrote in 1924, "Man will become immeasurably stronger, wiser and subtler; his body will become more harmonized, his movements more rhythmic, his voice more musical. The forms of life will become dynamically dramatic. The average human type will rise to the heights of an Aristotle, a Goethe, or a Marx. And above this ridge new peaks will rise."

In light of the Soviet Union's history of violence, imminent threats of civil war, a failed coup, and an economy in shambles, such words seemed mocking. Today, any Russian would laugh out loud at Trotsky's prediction. The *Pravda* editors were shaken to the core, so much so that they were now meeting with nineteen emissaries of a religion their founder had scorned as "the opiate of the people," asking us for help. "Christian values may be the only thing to keep our country from falling apart," said the editor-in-chief of *Pravda*.

I recalled an article I had read in *Atlantic Monthly* in 1989. "Can We Be Good Without God?" asked Glenn Tinder in the cover story, echoing the famous line from Dostoyevsky. Tinder's conclusion was, No. Apart from a higher moral code before which every political leader, no matter how powerful, must bow, and apart from an infusion of love that transmutes human selfishness into Christian charity and selflessness, a society will gradually but inevitably tilt toward chaos on the one hand or tyranny on the other. The Soviet Union, which had tried harder than any other nation to be "good" without God, had had its fill of tyranny. Now, what would keep it from chaos?

The editors of *Pravda* remarked wistfully that Christianity and communism have many of the same ideals. Some have even called communism a "Christian heresy" because of its emphasis on equality, sharing, justice, and racial harmony. But "seventy-four years on the road to nowhere," which is how Russians derisively refer to their Marxist past, have taught that the grandest social experiment in human history was terribly flawed.

Classical Marxists preached atheism and fought fiercely against religion for a shrewd reason: In order to inspire workers to rise up violently against their oppressors, Marxists had to kill off any hope in a heavenly life beyond this one, and any fear of divine punishment.

A Romanian pastor named Josif Ton once wrote of the contradiction that lies at the heart of a Marxist view of humanity. "[They teach] their pupils that life is the product of chance combinations of matter, that it is governed by Darwinian laws of adaptation and survival, and that it is man's only chance. There is no after-life, no 'savior' to reward self-sacrifice or to punish egoism or rapacity. After the pupils have been thus taught, I am sent in to teach them to be noble and honorable men and women, expending all their energies on doing good for the benefit of society, even to the point of self-sacrifice.

They must be courteous, tell only the truth, and live a morally pure life. But they lack motivation for goodness. They see that in a purely material world only he who hurries and grabs for himself possesses anything. Why should they be self-denying and honest? What motive can be offered them to live lives of usefulness to others?"

The *Pravda* editors conceded that they were having a hard time motivating people to show compassion. The average Soviet citizen would rather spend his money on drink than support needy children. A recent poll had revealed that 70 percent of Russian parents would not allow their children to have contact with a disabled child; 80 percent would not give money to help; some advocated infanticide. "How do you reform, change, motivate people?" the editors asked us. Early experiments in capitalism were not going well either because salespeople were surly and disinterested. The whole country seemed in a state of depression and despair.

"Everyone is looking for a society so perfect that people don't have to be good," said T. S. Eliot, who saw many of his friends embrace the dream of Marxism. What we were hearing from Soviet leaders, and the KGB, and now *Pravda*, was that the Soviet Union ended up with the worst of both: a society far from perfect, and a people who had forgotten how to be good.

I am perplexed by my own data and my conclusion is a direct contradiction of the original idea with which I start. Starting from unlimited freedom, I arrive at unlimited despotism. I will add, however, that there can be no solution of the social problem but mine.

— Fyodor Dostoyevsky,
The Possessed

CHAPTER NINE

The Last Marxist in Moscow

The day after our meeting with a subdued *Pravda*, a direct and challenging confrontation with Marxist ideology finally came our way on a visit to the Academy of Social Sciences. The name is misleading: until the August coup the Academy functioned as the preeminent finishing school for Marxist-Leninist leaders. Raisa Gorbachev once taught there, and many world leaders from the former Socialist bloc have studied at this elite school.

Like everything else in Russia, the Academy is undergoing tumultuous change. Until the fall of 1991 it received generous funding from the Communist party, but shortly before our visit subsidies were abruptly cut off. The Academy's professors, once coddled and privileged, now literally had no idea where their next paychecks would come from.

I had grown accustomed to the shabby look of most Moscow buildings. Pre-revolutionary buildings retained a certain charm, but most had peeling paint and wallpaper. Modern buildings, such as the one that housed *Pravda*, looked like winners in a "Design the ugliest building!" contest. Inside most government buildings, long dim hallways connected a warren of cubbyhole offices, each furnished with standard-issue desks and chairs. The Academy of Social Sciences, in sharp contrast, looked as if it had been helicoptered in intact from Scandinavia. Former United Nations ambassador Jeane Kirkpatrick on a recent visit had commented, "It's the only place I saw in Russia that looked like it had a landlord."

How could such luxury be lavished on a university? I wondered as our bus pulled into the towering marble complex. The hall we visited reminded me of the Kennedy Center in Washington. Enormous crystal chandeliers hung from a forty-foot ceiling, giving off enough candlepower to light the Moscow Airport several times over. An enclosed courtyard with a fountain and tropical plants dominated the foyer, designed so that the eye moved immediately to an imposing statue of Lenin carved out of gleaming white stone. A freestanding marble staircase curved up toward plush offices and meeting rooms.

Gawking like tourists, we climbed the marble stairway to the auditorium where Academy professors awaited us. The auditorium also had chandeliers; its walls were covered partly with wood paneling and partly with gilded wallpaper that would have looked more appropriate in the Palace of Versailles. Conference tables made of dark tropical woods formed a long U-shape, and fifty professors were assembled around the tables. Each place at the table was wired for simultaneous translation in several languages, and state-of-the-art video cameras mounted on the walls recorded the event for posterity.

Much like *Pravda*, the Academy of Social Sciences in its scramble to survive was reaching out to Christians, who still had some credibility with a restive populace. A parade of notables from American Christendom had recently visited, and the Academy was negotiating to establish a department for the study of Christianity.

As the dialogue with Academy professors proceeded, I sensed the same confusion we had seen in the *Pravda* editors. Of all people in the Soviet Union, these professors were true believers. Fed Communist theory practically from birth, they had devoted their lives to the propagation of it. One could still see relics of that intense devotion in the quasi-religious signs posted around Russia: "Lenin Lived. Lenin Lives. Lenin Will Live."

The professors recognized they had lost, perhaps forever, the battle of ideas. The cherished Marxist dream was over. They wanted to appear open to new ideas, such as capitalism and a free press, but the changes they had seen so far hardly seemed like improvements. In Moscow capitalism flourished mainly on Arbat Street, where teenagers employed by the Russian mafia exploited foreign tourists, the only people with hard currency. The soft-porn magazines springing up—*Playboy* had just inaugurated a Russian edition—as well as American television programs now available by satellite chilled them. Their daughters were talking about becoming hard-currency hookers, their sons were scheming for profits on the black market. Where was the ethics in this new freedom? they asked us.

Freedom scared them, and yet they could not deny its benefits. One Academy historian, borrowing from Tocqueville, mentioned the two streams that can issue from a common source of revolution: one leads to free arrangements among citizens, the other leads to absolute power.

"We started with common ideals," he said. "Leaders of both our societies talked about justice and equality and individual rights. Yet somehow you have produced a society that with all its problems still conveys courtesy and civility. I have been to the United States, and I see the difference even in the faces of your shopkeepers. Your minorities protest against discrimination—but they do not secede or start civil wars.

"Somehow, beginning from similar ideals, we have produced a society of beasts. We have murdered our own citizens in the name of the state. We know that we must move toward liberal democracy, but we don't know how. We no longer know what values to build a society upon."

Most groups in Moscow plied us eagerly with questions. The Academy professors seemed more anxious to talk. Listening to them, I felt I was in a political therapy session, nodding my head sympathetically as neurotic clients let long-suppressed anxieties spill out. It felt good to be listening for a change, after all the talking we had done.

In the midst of this genteel discussion, one of the Marxist professors, a specialist in philosophy, rose to his feet and asked for the floor (all other speakers had remained seated). Blotches of red appeared on his face, and as soon as he began speaking anger gushed forth. Others in the room looked around anxiously, concerned that he was straying from the mannerly dialogue. But there was no stopping this man. He had come to deliver a speech—a diatribe, really—not to fraternize with the enemy.

The Academy translator valiantly struggled to keep pace for a while, then waved for the professor to slow down, and finally gave up entirely. Russian-speakers in our group did their best to fill in, but the philosopher never paused to allow them to catch up.

We managed to grasp enough words to get the essence of his argument. "We need not have God to have morality!" he said. "Erich Fromm developed a fine morality based on Man with a capital 'M.' God is not necessary. Why pretend there is a God?"

The philosopher's volume rose and his face grew even more flushed. He punctuated the air with his finger as he made each point, and I thought of the paintings of Lenin addressing the workers. I thought too of stump preachers in the South where I had grown up. Of course! This man was a fanatic evangelist, the last true-blue, dyed-in-the-wool Marxist in Moscow. He was out to gain converts, and it mattered not at all if he was the last person in the world to believe these things. He was a bitter, wounded atheist, and he seized the chance to strike back.

"Marxism has not failed!" he shouted. "Yes, Stalin made mistakes. Yes, even our beloved Lenin made mistakes. Perhaps even Marx made mistakes. But go back to the young Marx, not the old Marx. There you will find the purity of the Socialist vision. There you will find a morality based on Man with the capital 'M.' That is what we need. As for Christianity, we already tried that in Russia—for one thousand years we tried it."

We members of Project Christian Bridge were fidgeting in our seats. Being yelled at by a fanatic is not a pleasant sensation, I realized, and tucked away the thought for further reflection. I whispered to the person next to me, "The problem with the young Marx is that he keeps turning into the old Marx." A few other members of our group were whispering to their seat-mates, and still others were clearing their throats, ready to jump in with a rebuttal.

The philosopher went on for ten or fifteen minutes until finally the emcee forced him to stop. I sensed in the atmosphere of the room an odd mixture of revenge and embarrassment. The professors waited for our response, and I cringed at the possibilities. Some of us weren't far removed from stump preachers ourselves, I knew, and the last thing the Academy needed was a wounded evangelical doing battle with a wounded atheist. By the providence of God, it was Kent Hill, director of the Institute on Religion and Democracy, who got the floor.

Kent Hill looks more professorial than the profes-sors. He wears glasses, has a scholarly demeanor, and speaks in soft, measured tones, the epitome of rational discourse. He also has a Ph.D. in Russian studies and was a Fulbright scholar in Moscow before taking the position at IRD. I did not envy him the spotlight he had just stepped into, but I could not imagine a finer repre-sentative to respond on our behalf.

"First, I want to affirm your right to your beliefs," Kent began, and waited respectfully for the translator to plug in his microphone and resume his work. "I am concerned about intolerance in the Soviet Union today—intolerance of atheists. I recently learned of an incident where a group allowed a Christian believer to speak, but shouted down an atheist. We have not come in that spirit. We support freedom of religion, and that includes freedom for those who do not believe in God."

Tension rushed from the room as if someone had opened an air lock. The professors nodded approval, and even the philosopher gave a curt nod. Kent continued.

"The issues you have raised tonight, sir, are impor-tant issues. In fact, I cannot think of more important issues to discuss. You have touched on questions of ultimate meaning for humanity and for the universe. Our group has thought long and hard about these questions. We have reached some conclusions, and we would love to discuss those with you.

"But one night's discussion would hardly do justice to these issues. I do not feel comfortable presenting a brief response. Could I make a suggestion? My family and I are moving to Moscow in December, and I will be teaching a course in Christian Apologetics at Moscow State University. I will gladly return to your Academy with Christian friends and set up a forum in which we can consider these important matters."

Again, nods of approval all around. Kent resumed, "But since I have the floor, I would like to mention why I believe the way I do." At this point, Kent lapsed into fluent Russian. The professors, some with looks of astonishment on their faces, removed their headphones and now we English-speakers were the ones listening to the simultaneous translation.

Kent told of a time of doubt in his life when he was tempted to abandon his Christian beliefs. He began reading Dostoyevsky's great novel *The Brothers Karamazov*— at this mention, more nods—which touches on many of the issues raised by the Academy philosopher.

"At first I found myself attracted to Ivan, the agnostic. His arguments against God were powerful, especially those concerning the problem of evil. I sensed in him a sincerity and a brilliant mind. As I read Dostoyevsky's book, I found myself gradually losing faith. But to my surprise, I was eventually won over by the love shown by Ivan's brother, Alyosha. Ivan had fine arguments, but he had no love. He could reason his way to a morality, but he could not create the love necessary to fulfill it. Eventually, I came to believe in Christ because I found in him a source for that love."

With that, Kent Hill sat down, and our meeting with the Academy of Social Sciences was transformed.

It occurred to me as we drove away from the ghostly marble buildings that Kent Hill had done far more than defuse one awkward confrontation. He had given us a model of evangelism for the shattered Soviet empire, perhaps the only model that will authentically work. First, he had begun with a genuine respect for the Soviets' own beliefs, even those diametrically opposed to his own. Unlike the philosophy professor, he had listened with courtesy and compassion before speaking.

Next, by moving to Moscow, Kent had committed himself to incarnational ministry. By themselves, no delegations of foreigners visiting for a week or a month will bring long-term change to the country. But a sprinkling of dedicated people who share the hardships and the turmoil, people willing to stand shoulder-to-shoulder in the Moscow bread lines, could perhaps become the salt that savors the whole society.

Finally, Kent pointed to the source of truth latent in the Russian culture itself. His lapse into the Russian language, almost instinctive as his response turned personal, and his reference to Dostoyevsky communicated far more to that audience than if he had quoted an entire epistle from the New Testament.

It was also through reading Dostoyevsky that Solzhenitsyn first began to understand the primacy of the spiritual over the material, a revelation which ultimately led to his conversion experience in a labor camp. Then Solzhenitsyn, too, became a directional signal pointing the way back toward God. As Kent Hill had so gently revealed, the seeds of renewal already lay in Russian soil.

What has happened with us? Who and for which transgressions has plunged us into this abyss of evil and misfortunes? Who has extinguished the light of virtue in our souls . . . the sacred light of our consciousness? We used to live with light in our souls . . . without scratching out the eyes of our neighbors, without breaking our neighbor's bones. Why has all this been abducted from us, and replaced by godlessness? . . . To whom are we going to turn our prayers now . . . to ask forgiveness?

— *Victor Astafev,*
"Place of Action"

CHAPTER TEN

Awakenings

In his book *Awakenings*, Dr. Oliver Sacks relates the case histories of twenty patients who lived in a suspended state of motionlessness and lowered metabolism brought about by a "sleeping sickness," encephalitis. Sacks discovered that the drug L-DOPA had a remarkable effect on such patients. A woman named Rose, semi-conscious for forty-three years, came to life, began moving her arms and legs, talked, and resumed contact with the world around her.

Everyone reacted to the drug a little differently, though. A few people realized an almost total cure, and were able to recommence a normal life. Others, like Leonard (the character played by Robert DeNiro in the movie version) experienced a brief and dramatic remission that ended when their bodies proved intolerant of L-DOPA. They had a few weeks of conversation, of walking outdoors, of dancing in the moonlight, before they lapsed again into a "frozen," immobile state.

In a case study published elsewhere, Sacks tells of a third response. Uncle Toby had sat silent in a corridor for seven years, his metabolic rate reduced to near zero. His body temperature hovered around thirty degrees below normal, yet with food and water he somehow stayed alive: "Alive, but not alive; in abeyance, in cold storage," as Dr. Sacks puts it. After a month's treatment with a thyroid drug, Uncle Toby awakened. Amazingly, he could walk and talk, although he had no memory of the previous seven years. Doctors, Uncle Toby's family, and Uncle Toby himself rejoiced at this Lazarus-like miracle. But something else awakened, too: a highly malignant carcinoma in Uncle Toby's chest, inactive for the past seven years, unexpectedly sprang to life. Uncle Toby died, in a fit of coughing, a few days after his awakening.

Which direction will the Soviet Union—even the term is anachronistic now—go? On my visit last fall, I saw signs of awakening everywhere. Vendors sold merchandise openly on Arbat Street; Pizza Hut, McDonald's, and other franchises were moving in; the government was reconverting seven thousand ancient churches, used as garages and warehouses, into places of worship. Muscovites danced in the moonlight. How long would the dance last? Was it only a brief remission before the disease broke loose again?

Russia does not have an encouraging history. "Tyranny is a habit which may be developed until at last it becomes a disease," wrote Dostoyevsky. A century later Solzhenitsyn added, "Left to ourselves, with only the help of the spherical object pivoted on the neckbone, we are more likely than not to take the wrong road." Whatever a people will submit to, a tyrant will arise to exploit, and Russia has a long pattern of submission. Some muttered darkly that Boris Yeltsin was such a tyrant: a throwback to the past, a malignancy unfrozen by a three-day August awakening.

Mass confusion reigns, as reflected daily in news stories from Moscow. Our last night there, our own delegation got a small taste of the kind of turmoil that prevails. We were staying in a splendid hotel that had formerly belonged to the Central Committee. When the Communist party was disgraced after the coup, the state government took over such properties—or so it thought. Upon checking into the hotel, we received identity cards marked "Guests of the President," and got assurances that the government would pick up the cost of our rooms. But when time came to pay the bill, the hotel demanded hard currency.

Several times over the next few days we witnessed the bizarre scene of a personal aide to President Gorbachev arguing with the hotel manager over who owned the fourteen-story structure. "It's our hotel, it belongs to the government!" the aide contended. "Fine, then pay the bill with government funds. But we only accept hard currency," the manager shot back, unyielding.

The night of our departure, this argument went on for four hours, finally ending at 2:00 A.M. in a compromise. The hotel agreed to accept two-thirds of the payment in rubles, but demanded one-third in hard currency. Gorbachev's government had no dollars even to issue its own ambassadors, and the humiliated aide had no choice but to turn to us for help. Fortunately, some of the veterans in our group, anticipating just such a problem, had brought along a large amount of cash. They knocked on doors in the middle of the night and collected the remainder of what was needed—$7000—so that we could depart the hotel.

Similar scenarios play out a thousand times each day. Who owns any building? For more than seventy years there has been no such thing as "private property" there. In a literal sense, the whole country is up for grabs.

In *Crime and Punishment* Dostoyevsky writes of the perilous sensation of living on one square yard of a cliff, on a narrow ledge where two feet can hardly stand, surrounded on all sides by an abyss, the ocean, everlasting darkness, everlasting solitude, and an everlasting storm. A good image for Russia and its neighbors, I decided. Everyone knows the danger on all sides; no one knows how to get off the cliff. Soon, very soon, the nation will have to step off the one square yard of cliff.

The day after the hotel fiasco our Lufthansa jet took off, lifting above the cloud cover, and I had my final glimpse of Russia. Already I was feeling the shock of reentry: I caught myself staring at the warm, expressive face of the flight attendant—a German at that—as she smilingly interacted with the passengers, distributing blankets, pillows, and headphones with a combination of professionalism and courtesy such as I had not seen since entering the country.

I arrived back in the United States on the seventy-fourth anniversary of the Bolshevik takeover, an event that has defined much of the history of the twentieth century. Television news reported that for the first time no official parades were held in Moscow. Later that week Boris Yeltsin banned most Communist party activities from Russian soil, thereby writing what may be the final chapter of the grand experiment.

What went wrong? Every day the news media report symptoms of a fatally flawed economic system. Curiously, I have not seen one mention in the media of what every Soviet leader insisted to us: the gravest crisis is not economic or political, but rather moral and spiritual. The failure of Marxism, we were told again and again, is above all a *theological* failure.

In his Templeton Address in 1983, Alexander Solzhenitsyn said, "Over half a century ago, while I was still a child, I recall hearing a number of older people offer the following explanation for the great disasters that had befallen Russia: 'Men have forgotten God; that's why all this has happened.' Since then I have spent well-nigh fifty years working on the history of our revolution; in the process I have read hundreds of books, collected hundreds of personal testimonies, and have already contributed eight volumes of my own toward the effort of clearing away the rubble left by that upheaval. But if I were asked today to formulate as concisely as possible the main cause of the ruinous revolution that swallowed up some sixty million of our people, I could not put it more accurately than to repeat: 'Men have forgotten God; that's why all this has happened.' "

Solzhenitsyn went on to say, "I myself see Christianity today as the only living spiritual force capable of undertaking the spiritual healing of Russia." When he made those remarks, the USSR was still a superpower and Solzhenitsyn was widely assailed for his old-fashioned views. Now, less than a decade later our delegation heard almost the identical assessment from top leaders of the nation. Above any other nation, the Soviet Union endeavored to get along without God. "Religion will disappear," Marx flatly predicted, its quaint beliefs made obsolete by the New Socialist Man. But religion did not disappear, and no New Socialist Man emerged.

In this century a morality play has been conducted on grand scale, with catastrophic consequences. What lies ahead? On the airplane on the way home, various members of Project Christian Bridge tried to speculate.

We all sensed the enormity of change that has already come. The new openness toward religion exceeded what any of us might have hoped for. In that regard, the prayers of millions of Christians inside and outside Russia have been answered.

Joel Nederhood, a member of our delegation, had this response, "Very few times in life do you get to sense the epic, the magnificent work of God. I believe that in our week together we experienced the epic. We saw a foretaste of Philippians 2, 'At the name of Jesus every knee shall bow.' God is doing something magnificent in Russia."

I, too, sensed the epic, and yet I confess that I tend toward realism, and hope does not come easily for me. I can hardly envision what a reconstituted, much less redeemed, Soviet Union would look like.

One thing only gives me hope. I will never forget the expressions on the faces of Basil, and the teenage prisoners in Zagorsk, and the woman television newscaster, and even the vice chairman of the KGB. Jesus' parables about the kingdom and the fig tree and the great banquet make one truth explicit: God goes where he is wanted. He does not force himself on an individual or on a nation, whether it be first-century Jews or twentieth-century Americans. And as I look back on my visit to Russia, one impression lingers above all others: never in my life have I been among people with a more ravenous appetite for God.

Project Christian Bridge

The following was Project Christian Bridge's response to the Supreme Soviets' plea for help from Christian leaders in the United States:

The individuals of Project Christian Bridge come from a variety of Christian organizations. Our delegation includes educators, religious leaders, broadcasters, missionaries, scholars, and social workers. We are not coming to promote Americanism or capitalism, though we appreciate our country and are aware of the benefits free markets have provided. In fact, we are profoundly aware of our national shortcomings and are fearful that our national religious heritage is being undermined. The message of Project Christian Bridge transcends national loyalty and political and economic views. We unashamedly advocate Christian understandings of reality—understandings which transcend the differences between individuals of different religious persuasions.

Our purpose for coming is as follows:

1. To encourage understanding and facilitate cooperation between American Christians and the governments of the USSR, Russia, and Ukraine;

2. To promote Christian ideas and values as a means of positively influencing family life, social problems (alcoholism, crime, etc.), business ethics, education, democratic structures, humanitarian ventures, and charitable activities;

3. To support understanding and cooperation between Protestants, Orthodox, and Catholics;

4. To promote religious freedom and equality of rights for all religious groups.

We come in a spirit of friendship, committed to exploring ways we may assist the people of the USSR, Russia, and Ukraine in this time of pivotal transition in your society. Our desire to help springs from our Christian conviction that "faith without works is dead." Hence, we desire not only to share our beliefs, but also to demonstrate our concern by stimulating the Christian community to carry out acts of compassion. We are impressed with the openness in your society to discuss anew matters of ultimate significance such as man's relationship to God and the meaning and purposes of human existence.

We firmly believe that religious faith, particularly Christianity, is a source of meaning and values. Orthodox, Catholics, and Protestants ought to work together to encourage the spread of basic Christian understanding. We believe Christian faith promotes patience, forgiveness, and compassion, as well as honesty and diligence. Though we advance our views with conviction, we insist on freedom for those who do not share our religious ideas. Further, we believe it is possible to cooperate with nonbelievers on the basis of natural law and cooperation with all people of good will.

We come in friendship to learn and to serve, to receive and to give. It is our prayer that Project Christian Bridge will unite us in the pursuit of noble goals.

Dr. John B. Aker, Pastor
First Evangelical Free Church
Rockford, IL

Dr. John Bernbaum, Executive Vice-President
Christian College Coalition
Washington, DC

Dr. Lynn Buzzard, Director
Church State Resources Center
Professor of Law
Campbell University School of Law
Buies Creek, NC

Anita Deyneka, Director of Communciations and Research
USSR Ministries
Wheaton, IL

Peter Deyneka, President
USSR Ministries
Wheaton, IL

Rev. Martin DeHaan, President
Radio Bible Class
Grand Rapids, MI

Mr. Phil Downer, President
Christian Businessmen's Committee of USA
Chattanooga, TN

Dr. Brandt Gustavson, Executive Director
National Religious Broadcasters
Parsippany, NJ

Dr. Kent Hill, Executive Director
Institute on Religion and Democracy
Washington, DC

Mr. Paul H. Johnson, Vice Chairman
Moody Bible Institute
Chicago, IL

Rev. Alex Leonovich, President
Slavic Missionary Service, Inc.
Middlebush, NJ

Mr. Richard Mason, Vice President
Radio Bible Class
Grand Rapids, MI

Dr. Billy Melvin, Executive Director
National Association of Evangelicals
Carol Stream, IL

Mr. Mikhail Morgulis, President
Christian Bridge
Wheaton, IL

Dr. Joel Nederhood, Director of Ministries
The Back To God Hour
Palos Heights, IL

Mr. Ronald Nikkel, President
Prison Fellowship International
Washington, DC

Dr. Herbert Schlossberg, Project Director
Fieldstead Institute
Minneapolis, MN

Mr. John Van Diest, Vice President of Literature Ministries
Multnomah Press
Portland, OR

Mr. Philip Yancey, Editor-at-Large
Christianity Today, Inc.
Carol Stream, IL

APPENDIX B

What Western Christians Can Do to Help

From Kent Hill, *Turbulent Times in the Soviet Church*
(Portland, Ore.: Multnomah Press, 1991), 175-182.

N ever during the Soviet period have the opportunities been as great for Christians in the West to help their co-believers in the USSR. This appendix is a resource guide for responding to this unique open door.

There is a serious shortage of religious literature in the Soviet Union. In addition to a tremendous demand for more Bibles in many languages, there is a great need for theological works, training materials for preparing ministers and priests, and religious literature for children. Church ministries also could be aided considerably by many more video players, video tapes, audio cassettes, computers, and religious goods.

An excellent resource on parachurch organizations involved in ministry to countries of Eastern Europe and the USSR is Mark Elliott's *East European Missions Directory* (1989, 81 pages), available from the Institute for East-West Christian Studies ($25 with postage; address listed later in appendix). Elliott has identified over 185 public missions, 56 broadcasters, and 35 research, education, and public advocacy groups.

Space limitations allow me to list only a few of the many fine organizations that provide information on or are working in the Soviet Union. There are more Protestant than Catholic or Orthodox groups involved in supplying literature, but I have tried to identify the non-Protestant groups in parentheses whenever possible so members of those faith communities will know whom to contact. (Many of the Protestant groups distributing Bibles provide them to non-Protestants as well.)

Coordinating Christian Ministries in the Soviet Union

The explosion of opportunities and interest in Christian ministry to the Soviet Union has created an urgent need for the creation of a clearinghouse of information on opportunities, organization programs, and personnel available for long-term and short-term assignment. As a result of initial funding from World Vision and the Institute on Religion and Democracy, the USSR Christian Resource Center was founded in the spring of 1991 in Washington, D.C. For further information, contact:

Kent R. Hill
USSR Christian Resource Center
1331 H Street N.W., Suite 900
Washington, DC 20005

Also administratively located at the offices of the Institute on Religion and Democracy is the Coalition for Solidarity with Christians in the USSR. Founded in 1987, this interdenominational coalition of twenty-seven organizations seeks to promote cooperation and an exchange of information between groups. When necessary, the Coalition intercedes on behalf of Christians who are experiencing discrimination or persecution.

During 1991, the Lausanne Committee for World Evangelization launched a project titled "Eastern Europe/USSR Strategy Study." The purpose is to discover and publicize to churches and Christian organizations ways in which they may help send Christian resources and Scriptures to Eastern Europe and USSR. For further information, contact:

P.O. Box 300
Oxford OX2 9XB
United Kingdom
Tel: 011-44-865-749-070

Two other reputable organizations are:

Peter and Anita Deyneka   Slavic Missionary Service
USSR Ministries   P.O. Box 5001
Three Danada Square East   Middlebush, NJ 08875
Suite 236   Tel: 908-873-8981
Wheaton, IL 60187
Tel: 708-462-1739

Research Organizations

Keston College   Keston, USA
Keston Research   P.O. Box 1310
33a Canal Street   Framingham, MA 01701
Oxford, OX2 6BQ
United Kingdom
Tel: 011-44-865-311-022

General Director: Rev. Canon Michael Bourdeaux

Keston, USA is the American affiliate of Keston College in England, the foremost organization in the world for the study of religion in Communist countries. Keston was founded in 1969 by Michael Bourdeaux. It provides up-to-date information through *Keston News Service* (biweekly, $50 per year), *Keston FAX* ($125 per year), *Religion in Communist Lands* (quarterly, $30 per year, *Frontier* (bimonthly popular magazine, $15 per year), and the publication of books.

Institute for East-West Christian Studies
Wheaton College
Wheaton, IL 60187-5593
(708) 260-591

Director: Dr. Mark R. Elliott

The Institute for East-West Christian Studies assists Christian workers, scholars, and the Soviet Union and Central and Eastern Europe. In addition, the East-West Institute engages in research and facilitates Christian ministry in the Soviet Union and Central and Eastern Europe. The Institute realizes its mission through the acquisition, production, and dissemination of a wide range of resources and through sponsorship of various educational and inspirational forums.

Research Center for Religion and
Human Rights in Closed Societies
475 Riverside Drive
New York, NY 10115
(212) 870-2481 or 870-2440

Executive Director: Olga Hruby

Established in 1962, the Center holds conferences and publishes information, including its quarterly journal, *Religion in Communist Dominated Areas* (RCDA, $25 per year).

Religious Literature

In recent years, the Soviets have been allowing numerous packages of religious literature and other goods to reach their destinations by mail or in large shipments. Bibles and other religious literature may be obtained from the following organizations. If an individual sends in materials, it is best to send no more than three books in one package, preferably of different titles. Most will prefer simply to make a contribution to an organization.

Slavic Gospel Association
P.O. Box 1122
Wheaton, IL 60189
(708) 690-8900

American Bible Society
1865 Broadway
New York, NY 10023
(212) 408-1499

Open Doors/USA
P.O. Box 27001
Santa Ana, CA 92799
(714) 531-6000

Door of Hope International
P.O. Box 303
Glendale, CA 91209
(818) 956-7500

Light in the East
39 Pilgrim Way
Westburg, NY 11590
(516) 334-6792

Inst. for Bible Translation
Box 20100
S-10460 Stockholm
Sweden
Tel: 08-94-5414

World Bible Translation
    Center
P.O. Box 820648
Fort Worth, TX 76182
(817) 595-1664

Religious Books for
    Russia
P.O. Box 522
Glen Cove, NY 11542
(Orthodox)

Bibles for the World
P.O. Box 505
Wheaton, IL 60189
(708) 668-7733

International Bible Society
P.O. Box 62970
Colorado Springs, CO
    80962
(719) 488-9200

Eastern European Bible Mission
P.O. Box 110
Colorado Springs, CO 80901
(719) 577-4450

Other Mission and Service Ministries

Many of the groups listed above, such as Slavic Gospel Association, are also involved in religious education, evangelism, and in providing a wide variety of material resources needed by Christians and churches in the Soviet Union. Organizations which specialize in ministries that go beyond Bible distribution include:

Aid to the Church in Need
P.O. Box 576
Deer Park, NY 11729-0576
(Catholic)

Rise Foundation
7424 Piney Branch Rd
Tacoma Park, MD 20912
(Orthodox)

Issachar Frontier
Mission Strategies
19321 44th Ave. West, #204
Lynnwood, WA 98036
(206) 744-0400

Youth with a Mission
(Slavic Ministries)
P.O. Box 4213
Salem, OR 97302
(503) 363-1571

Operation Mobilization
P.O. Box 2277
Peachtree, GA 30269
(404) 631-0432

Mission Possible
P.O. Box 2014
Denton, TX 76202
(817) 382-1508

Christian Solidarity Int'l.
P.O. Box 70563
Washington, DC 20024
(301) 989-0298

Logos Bible Training
  by Extension
P.O. Box 409
Fresno, CA 93708-0409
(209) 291-6874

Lithuanian Catholic Religious Aid
351 Highland Boulevard
Brooklyn, NY 11207
(718) 647-2434

Radio Broadcasters

One of the most effective ways of helping Christians in the Soviet Union during the past difficult decades has been radio broadcasting. But the importance of radio is no less great today; in fact, the opportunities for the effective use of broadcasting have never been greater. These ministries depend heavily on the support of individual Christians and churches. There is much more that could be done if only the support were available to expand these vital ministries. Some of the better known broadcasters include:

International Russian
    Radio/TV
Box 225414
Dallas, TX 75222
(817) 354-8110

IBRT
Hannu Haukka
Box 71
04251 Kerava
Finland
(358) 0-2945400

Slavic Gospel Association
Nick Leonovich
P.O. Box 1122
Wheaton, IL 60189
(708) 690-8900

Russian Christian Radio
P.O. Box 1667
1732 Mountain View Court
Estes Park, CO 80517
(303) 586-8638

Far East Broadcasting Co.
Box 1
La Mirada, CA 90637
(213) 947-4651

Trans World Radio
International Headquarters
Box 700
Cary, NC 27512-0700
(919) 460-9596

Radio Vatican
00120
Vatican City
Italy

Holy Archangel
    Broadcasting
Center (Orthodox)
3770 39th Street NW
Washington, DC 20016
(202) 363-1602

Mennonite Brethren Communications
Victor Hamm   Voice of Orthodoxy
Box 2, Station F   P.O. Box 501
Winnipeg, Manitoba R2L 2A5   Tuckahoe, NY 10707
Canada
(204) 667-9576

Exchanges/Contacts

Christian Academic/Cultural.

A number of colleges and seminaries are now engaged in or have conducted exchanges with Soviet institutions. The Christian College Coalition, representing approximately eighty institutions of higher education, is a good source of information on opportunities which exist. Contact:

John Bernbaum
Vice President
Christian College Coalition
329 8th Street NE
Washington, DC 20002
(202) 546-3086

The International Institute for Christian Studies is establishing departments of Christian studies at secular educational institutions in Eastern Europe and the USSR. Western Christian faculty who are interested in teaching in such a department can contact:

Daryl McCarthy
Executive Director
International Institute for Christian Studies
Box 13157
Overland Park, KS 66212
(913) 339-6530

Campus Crusade for Christ, International Teams/USA, and InterVarsity are involved in setting up academic/cultural exchanges or contacts. Contact:

Glen Tosaya
Campus Crusade
  for Christ
P.O. Box 62245
Colorado Springs, CO
  80962
(719) 593-0300

Mark K. Dyer
International
  Teams/USA
P.O. Box 203
Prospect Heights, IL
  60070
(708) 870-3800

Chuck Ellis
InterVarsity Christian Fellowship
6400 Schroeder Road
P.O. Box 7895
Madison, WI 53707-7895
(608) 274-9001

Much of Soviet society no longer identifies itself with religious belief, though it is open to contacts with Christians. The present situation is ideal for Western Christians to explore avenues of contact with their professional counterparts in the Soviet Union.

Helping Soviet Christians Who Leave the USSR

Sponsor a Refugee Family.

World Relief is the international humanitarian assistance arm of the National Association of Evangelicals. While there are ten national organizations contracted to sponsor and resettle refugees, World Relief is the only organization responsible for working primarily with the evangelical Christian denominations in resettling refugees in the United States.

The chief objective of the sponsor is to help the refugee to integrate quickly and successfully into

American society. The responsibilities of sponsoring a family include meeting their initial material needs (housing, clothing, food) as well as their spiritual and emotional needs (adjusting to the Western church, for example). If your church or community is interested in getting involved in a direct ministry to aid Soviet refugees, contact World Relief:

Soviet Refugee Project
World Relief
P.O. Box WRC
Nyack, NY 10960
(914) 268-4135

You also may wish to contact EXODUS World Service, which does good work providing information on refugee resettlement:

Dennis Ripley
EXODUS World Service
P.O. Box 7000
West Chicago, IL 60185-7000
(312) 733-8433

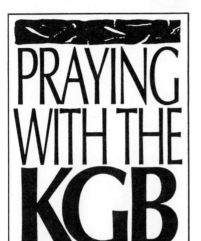

Dear reading Friend:

You are in for a *real* treat.
The day Philip Yancey sent me a copy of his latest book, I planned to look it over that evening and then spend more time digesting it at a later date. Less than four hours after I had sat down for that "quick glance," I finished the last page.

I found myself riveted to my chair as one story after another fascinated me to such an extent, I simply could not put it down. The changes in Russia are so sweeping that if you are like me, you will shake your head in amazement.

Rather than meeting up with a spirit of suspicion in those he encountered, Philip tells me he found them to be spiritually starved. And instead of their being closed and aloof, he and his friends were greeted with open arms.

May God use these pages to set your heart ablaze. Pray with us that we might have wisdom regarding the role IFL should play in this brand-new mission field.

Thank you,

Chuck

Insight for Living • Post Office Box 69000, Anaheim, CA 92817-0900
Insight for Living Ministries • Post Office Box 2510, Vancouver, BC, Canada V6B 3W7
Insight for Living, Inc. • GPO Box 2823 EE, Melbourne, VIC 3001, Australia